FINANCIAL FREEDOM ON $5 A DAY
A step-by-step strategy for small investors

Chuck Chakrapani, M.Sc., Ph.D., C.I.M.

Self-Counsel Press
(*a division of*)
International Self-Counsel Press Ltd.

Printed in Canada

First edition: March, 1983
Second edition: February, 1994
Third edition: January, 1986
Reprinted: September, 1986
Fourth edition: March, 1989
Fifth edition: April, 1991
Reprinted: July, 1991; May, 1992; September, 1993
Sixth edition: December, 1994
Reprinted: September, 1995; February, 1996

Canadian Cataloguing in Publication Data
    Chakrapani, Chuck
    Financial freedom on $5 a day

    (Self-counsel business series)
    ISBN 0-88908-794-6
    ISSN 0827-2522
    1. Investments — Periodicals. 2. Speculation — Periodicals.
      I. Title. II. Series.
    HG4527.C428   332.6'78   C84-031650-X

Cover photography by Lonnie Duka/Tony Stone Images

                        Self-Counsel Press
                        (*a division of*)
                International Self-Counsel Press Ltd.

    1481 Charlotte Road   1704 N. State Street
North Vancouver, British Columbia   Bellingham, Washington
            V7J 1H1   98225

CONTENTS

CHARTS

SAMPLES

PREFACE

This book describes a safe, long-term investment strategy. Even if you have no savings at the moment, even if you can save no more than $5 a day, you can achieve financial freedom using the techniques described in this book.

Most books on investing assume that you have several thousand dollars to invest. Unfortunately, this is not always true. Many of us do not have large savings. It is not easy to get investment advice when you do not have several thousand dollars to invest. Many investment advisers will not take the time to explain what you should do with your $300. There are no books on the market that will explain the options open to you.

This book is different. It tells you how you can invest, starting with as little as $100. The information is very specific. The book gives you the addresses and phone numbers of companies you can contact. It explains specific investments and tells you how you can get a piece of the action.

In this edition of the book, I have updated information, rewritten most chapters, and added a few new chapters. I hope you find it even more useful than the earlier editions.

Inevitably, there is a gap between the time the information is collected and the time it eventually reaches you. Therefore, no matter how much I have tried to make the book up-to-date, there will be some addresses and phone numbers that are out of date. If you are unsuccessful with a few addresses or phone numbers, don't be discouraged. There is enough information in this book to create your investment plan — a plan that will make you financially independent, slowly but surely.

This book does not distinguish between the Canadian and the U.S. dollar. Items that refer to the U.S. market are in U.S. dollars and items that refer to the Canadian market are in Canadian dollars. If you need $100 to join a U.S. mutual fund you need U.S. $100; if you need $100 to join a Canadian mutual fund you need Cdn. $100. Prices of gold and silver are, by tradition, in U.S. dollars.

The first edition of this book came out in 1983. Since then I have received literally hundreds of letters from readers telling me how useful they have found it. The information in this book takes a long time to compile and such letters make me feel that this project is worthwhile. Thank you.

The amount of research that goes into a book of this nature requires the help of several people. It is impossible to thank everyone individually. However, one person deserves special thanks: Christine Mole, who assisted me in every way in putting together this edition of the book.

A Personal Statement

I have written over ten books. But *Financial Freedom on $5 a Day* gives me the greatest satisfaction. Basic books on investing have a notoriously short life. So it pleases me to note that, with your support, this book has been continuously in print for more than ten years.

Most authors look for endorsement of their work from celebrities and famous people. To me, the most meaningful endorsement comes from my readers. They have read it, used it, and found that it delivers what it claims. I would like to quote just two letters out of the hundreds in our files. (These are unsolicited testimonials written by readers; the originals can be viewed at the Standard Research Systems offices by prior appointment.)

> At 45, after 20 years of marriage, we had no savings, no investments...Sixty days after buying your book I have $700 split between

two investments and $1,000 in savings. The "Ten Plus Principle" alone was worth the cash of the book many times over. Thank you! Thank you!

Mrs. N.K., West Palm Beach, Florida

I bought your book in the early eighties when I was broke. Then I started saving $5 a day from your ideas in the book. I saved enough to buy a duplex for $35,000... We put $10,000 into the property, now it is worth $150,000. I paid my mortgage off in 1989 and bought my second home on the St. Lawrence River for $90,000. Now after two years of hard work, it is worth $175,000... I have just bought your new book for myself and my son and am looking for new ways of investing. Thanks! Your book was a great help to me and other people I have helped with saving money.

Mr. J.E. Brockville, Ontario

I do not want to pretend that I wrote this book for purely altruistic reasons. Among other things, I am an author by profession. But one of my motives for writing this book is to help small investors who cannot get such help elsewhere. It pleases me a great deal to know that it made a difference in a few people's lives and they cared to share it with me.

I hope it makes a difference in your life and I wish you the very best.

PART I
FINANCIAL FREEDOM:
YOU CAN ACHIEVE IT

1
YOU CAN ACHIEVE FINANCIAL FREEDOM

a. EVEN SMALL INVESTORS CAN ACHIEVE FINANCIAL FREEDOM

What if I told you that within a year from today you could have:

- investments in the stock market
- investments in bonds
- international investments
- some gold and silver
- equity in real estate

and much more? Would you believe it?

Whether you believe it or not, you can have all these and even more. All you need is to put the ideas described in this book into practice. Many people have already done it. I have had many letters from people who read earlier editions of this book and put into practice what they read. Many of them started with practically no savings. Yet, by now, they are financially independent. Or they are on their way to becoming so.

The ideas presented are simple but powerful. There are no gimmicks in this book. Instead, you will find many no-nonsense ideas regarding investments that have high profit potential.

You have probably always suspected that there are highly profitable investments open to the small investor. But how can you find out about them? After all, most investment advisers are after big money. They are not interested in telling you how to wisely invest your first $100.

The result? Most small investors remain in the dark about the opportunities open to them. Small investors continue to be small investors, while large investors continue to increase their wealth.

Help is on the way! This book is written to show you how to build wealth, even if you don't have any savings now. North America is still a land of opportunities. If you ever dream about becoming financially free, your dream can become reality.

Several years ago when I started investing, no one told me that wonderful opportunities existed for the small investor. I wasted many years pursuing useless advice. Investment books provided little usable advice for the small investor.

If you are in the same position as I was several years ago, let me assure you, you are much better off than I was. You hold in your hands a book that tells you:

- how to set up an investment program that does not require mountains of cash to start

- how to begin today — not after you have saved enough money to invest. A book that takes the mystery out of investing and makes investing understandable and fun!

- how to set up a successful investment program that works automatically and with little or no risk

- how to be your own financial consultant so you understand and manage your money

I know that the principles contained in this book, simple as they may be, work. They have worked for me and they have worked for many people over the years.

4

b. WHY AREN'T MOST PEOPLE FINANCIALLY INDEPENDENT?

Most people in our society would like to be financially independent, but unfortunately most of us are not. If, as I believe, North America is still a land of opportunities, why aren't most of us financially independent?

I know we can all be financially independent. I will prove it to you by the time you finish reading this book. For the time being, just assume that anyone who wants to be financially free can be. Then why aren't most people financially independent? Why can't about 95% of North Americans fully support themselves when they retire?

The reason is simple. We all want the good life. But we are not prepared to do what it takes to achieve it. *Doing whatever it takes to get there is the secret of success,* in investing as in life. It is unfortunate that most people do not do what it takes to achieve financial freedom. Most people don't realize this, but what you need to do is simple and straightforward. As this book suggests, start today with $5, put aside $5 every day, add to it as time goes on, and invest wisely. That is all it takes.

Yet most of us do not do what it takes to get to financial independence. We hope. We procrastinate. We hesitate. We wait for the magic day when we will have the "money to invest." When we invest, we do so on the spur of the moment with no rhyme or reason. We do not start with a plan.

To achieve financial freedom you need a plan. You are unlikely to achieve financial freedom by random investments or by daydreaming. Even hard work may not get you there. Just as you cannot hope to end up with a house by building walls without a plan, so you cannot hope to achieve financial freedom without a plan. Many investors do not achieve financial freedom because they work without a plan — they are simply building walls hoping that somehow they will end up with a house!

5

c. WHAT IT TAKES TO ACHIEVE FINANCIAL FREEDOM

Achieving financial freedom is not difficult. As I said earlier, anyone who wants it can achieve it. There are, in fact, four ingredients to financial success. They are the following:

(a) Regular savings, however small

(b) Patience and avoidance of greed

(c) A well-conceived plan of action

(d) Knowing where and how to invest

If you can look after the first two items, this book will assist you with the last two items: a plan of action and information on where and how to invest your money for healthy profits.

Investments should have a purpose. They should be made regularly. You need patience and you should avoid greed. Why are these things important? Without a purpose, you cannot make logical investment choices. Without patience, you may abandon your program halfway through. With greed, you are likely to lose all your money in some absurd scheme to get rich quickly. Avoid these traps. In fact, if you simply follow this book faithfully, you will automatically avoid these traps.

Will reading this book make you financially independent? Reading this book, or any other book for that matter, will not make you financially independent — unless you act upon its suggestions. It is not knowledge but *action* that makes people successful. To succeed, you should be prepared to put the principles described in this book into practice.

I have tried to make it easier for you to act on my suggestions. When I ask you to save, I discuss how to save. When I suggest that you consider a particular investment, I have included contact addresses and phone numbers. When

6

I say you should find out more, I have listed what you should read. In fact, this book contains practically everything you need to know. I hope that this book will take you from wherever you are now to financial freedom.

But — and I cannot emphasize this strongly enough — whether you become financially independent or not will depend not on whether you read this book, but on your motivation to act on the suggestions it contains.

The program explained in this book requires your involvement and commitment for you to succeed. With your involvement and commitment, you are on your way to financial freedom. Can you pay yourself $5 a day to start and spend 30 minutes a month reviewing your investments? If you can, it is virtually certain that you will achieve financial freedom in the next few years.

d. DREAM MERCHANTS: DO YOU WANT TO PAY THEM?

The world of investing is full of dream merchants. Out in the world are many people who are desperate to help you — for a small consideration of just a few (or a few hundred) dollars. Their message is the same: "give me some money *now* and I will tell you how to get rich *later*." In various forms, here are their messages:

- Start a mail order business with no capital.

- Buy real estate with no money down.

- Buy the stocks I suggest and multiply your money.

- Buy gold futures, pork bellies or whatever.

- Use pyramid schemes and get rich in 30 days.

These are the conservative ones! The more extreme ones tell you how to pick the winning number in a lottery, buy coins and paintings (that *they* sell), play blackjack, use a "surefire" betting system, think rich, or get involved in a chain letter scheme.

Do they work?

I don't know of anyone who got rich by using a system to pick winning numbers in a lottery. If indeed there were such a system, why are they trying to sell it to us instead of using it themselves so they can spend the rest of their lives getting tanned under the sun by the sea?

Chain letters (which are generally illegal) can make you money if *you* start them and have the good fortune to find a number of gullible people to go along with the scheme. I hope you don't get arrested before you get rich!

In general, you shouldn't be learning the secrets of getting rich from someone who is desperate to let you in on the secret for $10. It is more likely that the money you pay will pay someone else's grocery bills rather than make you rich.

How about the more respectable schemes?

You can indeed make money in the mail order business. But it is hard work and success is by no means guaranteed. Besides, despite claims to the contrary, you will need some capital. While the mail order business has several advantages, it can be tough. It is unrealistic to expect it to be easy to make money in the mail order business. I know — I have sold several items through the mail.

You can also make money in real estate — but not necessarily with ease. Perhaps you know of people who got hurt speculating in real estate. I do.

There are many people in both the mail order and the real estate business who never got rich and probably never will. In any case, despite the extravagant claims of the advertisements, these businesses are not really "get-rich-quick" schemes. They are legitimate businesses with high profit potential. The qualities to succeed in these ventures are similar to the ones you would need to succeed in any other business — hard work, sufficient capital, perseverance, etc.

So what's left?

One could speculate on gold or oil (for example by buying gold in the futures market). Such schemes can work. But what happens to your money will depend on what the gnomes of Zurich and the Saddam Husseins of this world decide to do. For example, if you bought gold futures in early 1979 (and pyramided the profits), you would have become a millionaire by 1980. But if you had bought gold futures in 1980 and pyramided the profits, you would have probably gone bankrupt. Again, you would have made virtually no money by speculating in oil prices in 1989, but you could have made spectacular profits if you had started speculating (in the right direction) in 1990, just before Iraq invaded Kuwait.

Some get-rich-quick schemes work and some don't. Those that do, do not work consistently. Many schemes carry a high level of risk. It is my view that get-rich schemes are simply not suitable for most investors — whether large or small, beginning, or sophisticated. It is better to get rich slowly than to get poor in a hurry.

e. GETTING RICH SLOWLY BUT SURELY

Now that we have dismissed get-rich schemes, can a small investor, starting with no capital, really get rich? The answer is yes. Any investor can make enough money to become financially free. It takes discipline, patience, and a little effort. And it takes time. But it can be done. If you have enough money to buy this book and if you are sincerely willing to put what is described into practice, you probably have all it takes to achieve financial freedom!

The techniques described in this book will not make you rich overnight. But they will lead you to financial freedom in the next few years. As I said earlier, you need a certain amount of patience, discipline, and effort. This does not mean that you have to sacrifice your present happiness to achieve future financial freedom. Slightly rewording *Alice in Wonderland*, what we need is jam today *and* jam tomorrow!

It is meaningless to suffer today so you can be happy sometime in the future. Today is as important as any other day of your life. The program in this book is designed in such a way that you can carry it out without feeling that you have to forego the essential things you need now.

You will need some discipline, but let me assure you, it will not cramp your style! After all, you are not likely to achieve financial freedom if you do not plan and if you are unwilling to change your habits a bit. Getting rich does not demand that we make ourselves miserable now. It does mean, however, that we make some gentle changes in the way we spend and save.

Although the program described here will work for all types of investors, I have designed it specially for investors who —

- do not want to start and run a business,
- believe that there is no such thing as a free lunch,
- do not want to take undue risks with his or her money, and
- would rather invest $10 wisely than pay hundreds of dollars for a get-rich-quick scheme.

f. IS IT STILL $5 A DAY?

It is over ten years since this book first came out. With all the inflation since then, are we still talking about $5 a day? Should we increase it to *Financial Freedom on $10 a Day*? Here is the good news: it is still $5 a day!

What stops most people from achieving financial freedom is the idea that they have to have a lot of money to get started. So start with any amount. Five dollars a day is good enough.

If you can't afford even that, start with even less. See for yourself how easy it is to build an investment plan and how well your money grows. Once you have done that, you will find ways to increase your daily investment to the extent you can afford. If you stick with the plan even for a couple of years, you will begin to see the results you like. By then, you will be thinking of new ways to save and invest. You will not be finding excuses to avoid investing.

g. FIVE DOLLARS A DAY GETS YOU STARTED

Financial freedom on $5 a day! Is it possible? The answer is yes and I will show you how.

Let's say that you are now 30 years old and that you plan to retire at 65. If you can save just $5 a day and invest for a 13% return, you will have well over $1,200,000 by the time you retire — even if you have no other savings and no other investment plan.

But of course you want to be financially independent long before you retire — unless you are already close to retirement. And it can be done. The point of the example is simply to show that you do not have to start with a lot of money to retire financially independent.

If you are willing to set aside a small amount each day, and if you are willing to be patient, you can achieve financial freedom. This book will show you how.

The program described in this book will work for you even if you do not know anything about investments, and even if you do not have a lot of savings now. I am assuming, however, that you are willing to be systematic and patient with your investments and will take the initiative to implement the program. Let's get busy! Five dollars a day gets you started. Today is the day to begin.

2
WHAT MAKES YOU WEALTHY?

a. WHAT IS FINANCIAL FREEDOM ANYWAY?

Financial freedom means different things to different people. For me, it means maintaining my current lifestyle through my investments without having to depend on other sources of income. Suppose you make $40,000 a year. Financial freedom is when you can make about $40,000 a year solely through your investments. If you can accumulate a capital of about $333,000 and invest it for an average return of 12%, then you will get $40,000 a year.

If you are sufficiently interested in putting the principles in this book into practice, chances are that you will be able to achieve financial freedom. The basic premise of the book is this: most people, regardless of their current situation, can achieve financial freedom. There might be obvious exceptions. If you are already 63 and have no savings but would like to achieve financial freedom by 65, it is unlikely that this book will make it happen. On the other hand, if you are in your early forties or even your fifties, and you are willing to make up for lost time there is no reason why you cannot achieve financial freedom or something close to it.

Financial freedom is not a "yes" or "no" condition. If you need $40,000 of investment income, but can make only $35,000 a year through your investments, you are still much better off than someone who is entirely at the mercy of government and private pensions.

So here it is. *The principles laid out in this book will help most people achieve financial freedom, regardless of their current situation.*

You may be tempted to say that you are too close to retirement, or that you are already retired, or that you have heavy personal debts. Even in these cases, I believe that putting the principles described in this book into practice will make your financial situation better than it would be otherwise.

b. HOW DO I GET THERE FROM HERE?

Maybe you are still skeptical. You are probably wondering how, starting from scratch, you can go from zero wealth to financial freedom. After all, in the first chapter I dismissed all "get-rich-quick" schemes as being unsuitable for small investors. In fact, I even suggested that you should avoid risking your money in your search for a higher return. If I say there are no magical solutions and if I don't promise you the moon, you may wonder how you are ever going to achieve financial freedom. Especially when I say that all you need to begin with is just $5 a day.

You have a right to be skeptical, and I hope you are. Skepticism is the best protection an investor has against the sharks that infest the sea of investment.

c. THREE POWERFUL PRINCIPLES

The program that I am about to describe incorporates three powerful principles of investing. These principles are powerful, though they may look deceptively simple.

1. The magic of compounding

If you invest $1,000 at 12% interest per year, you will have $2,000 in six years. But if you leave it for about 30 years, you will have $30,000, if you don't add a penny during all that time. During the first six years, your investment made only $1,000. But between the years 24 and 30, your investment made $15,000. When you invest, your money will grow faster and faster as time goes on. This is because money makes money, and the money that money makes, makes even more money. This is called "the magic of compounding." The Financial Freedom on $5 a Day strategy (3FD strategy for short) is a long-term strategy that takes full advantage of the principle of compounding.

One of the major mistakes in investing is made by young people. Nobody told them about the power of compound interest. So they postpone investing to some future date. This is a major mistake.

Let me illustrate. Joe invests $2,000 a year between the ages of 18 and 23 and does not invest any further. Jane starts at age 25 and invests $2,000 every year until her retirement at age 65. (Assume a return of 10% in both cases.) Who will have more money when they retire? Jane? Guess again.

Believe it or not, Joe's $10,000 investment would be worth $735,600 at retirement while Jane's $42,000 would be worth $531,111. Just because Joe had a few more years' compound return than Jane.

You are never too young to start investing. In fact, you can achieve spectacular returns if you start early, and the earlier the better.

But neither are you too old to start investing. Our strategy will work for anybody who wants to invest to build a secure future. Chart #1 shows how $5 a day would grow over an extended period of time.

2. Dollar cost averaging

Suppose you decide to buy an investment that goes up and down in price. Further, you decide to invest $100 every month on this investment. If the price of this investment for a given month is $10, you will buy ten units ($100/$10). If the price for the following month is $12.50, you will buy only eight units ($100/$12.50). If the price drops to $5, then you will buy 20 units ($100/$5). In other words, by investing the same amount every month, you buy more when the price is low and less when the price is high. In most situations, your

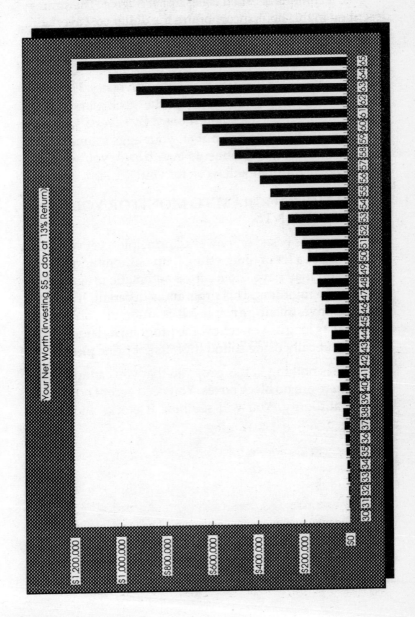

Your Net Worth (investing $5 a day at 13% Return)

30 31 32 33 34 35 36 37 38 39 40 41 42 43 44 45 46 47 48 49 50 51 52 53 54 55 56 57 58 59 60 61 62 63 64 65

$0 · $200,000 · $400,000 · $600,000 · $800,000 · $1,000,000 · $1,200,000

15

average price will turn out to be lower than what it would have been if you had not used this method.

This technique is called *dollar cost averaging*. The strategy described in this book incorporates the dollar cost averaging technique.

3. Diversification

Many investors lose because they fail to diversify. For example, they may put all their money in the stock market. If the market crashes, they lose their money. By diversifying, you make sure that you do not put all your eggs in one basket. Even if one of your investments goes down, you will have other investments that will work for you.

d. USE THE PROGRAM TO MONITOR YOUR INVESTMENTS

This program is based on powerful principles, yet you don't have to spend a lot of time setting it up or monitoring it. It is simple. You may have come across automatic programs before that are mindless. This program is different. It is based on sound investment principles. It is automatic only in the sense that as long as you follow the program as laid out, you are automatically using sound investment principles.

There is nothing in this program that you cannot understand. There are no black boxes. You need accept nothing on faith or authority. You will see how it works and why it works.

PART II
GETTING MONEY TO INVEST

3

HOW TO GET MONEY TO INVEST

a. PAY YOURSELF FIRST

Do you tell yourself that you will start saving and investing when you earn more? Many people do. Years go by, but the day never arrives. Their income has increased over the years, but so have their expenditures. They say to themselves that they will start saving when they earn even more! When they are about to retire, they wonder what they did with all their money over the years!

Simply put, if you wait for your income to increase before you start saving, you will probably never make it. You have to start saving now.

Today.

But how? How can you possibly save when you have no money left by the end of the month?

Wait a minute. You work hard for your money. You take care of all your bills — telephone, hydro, rent, household expenses, gifts. The list goes on. But did you pay yourself? When you have paid all your bills, what have you got left for yourself? Nothing? You have nothing to show for all your hard work? Are you saying that money simply passes through your hands and you have no control over it?

How can this be? I know how. Most people tend to plan backwards. Instead of paying themselves first, they pay others first. Then they find that there is nothing left.

This way of thinking has to change. Now. As Northcote Parkinson said, expenditure rises to meet income. This is why

19

you find that although your income has risen over the years, you have no significant savings. That is what is wrong in believing that at some future time you will be able save, but not now.

If you want to achieve financial independence, the first commandment is PAY YOURSELF FIRST. The amount you pay yourself may be small (like $5 a day), but you have to pay yourself first. When you pay yourself, you will automatically begin to adjust your other expenses.

"Easier said than done!" you may say. But think of the alternative. You have a choice. You can pay yourself first and look forward to a secure future or you can find excuses to avoid paying yourself and look forward to being strapped in your old age.

Let me assure you that there are simple and painless ways of saving. I describe them in the next section.

b. THREE SIMPLE WAYS TO SAVE

Different people save differently. In my opinion, there are three ways to save that are particularly simple. You can save by using any one of these three techniques:

(a) The Minus Ten technique

(b) The Plus Ten technique

(c) The Day's Due technique

You can use any method that appeals to you.

1. The Minus Ten technique

When you use this method, you arrange to have 10% of your salary deducted before it reaches you. For example, you can instruct your bank or trust company to transfer 10% of your salary every month to a (different) savings account. As far as you are concerned, the remaining 90% left in your regular account is all that is available for spending.

The 10% that is transferred to a different account is not your spending money, it is not your emergency money, it is not your holiday money — it is your investment money, the money that will make you financially independent.

2. The Plus Ten technique

This is my favorite technique. Whenever you spend money, set aside 10% of the money spent. For example, if you spend $500 on rent, set aside $50 toward saving. If you spend $1 on coffee, set aside a dime. Do this no matter how small or how large the expenditure is. Develop your "Plus Ten" thinking. This way, you'll automatically add 10% to all items; it is like adding your own tax so that you can be financially independent. If you want to buy an item that costs $100, think of it as costing you $110. That is the amount you need to buy the item. If you don't have it, you can't afford it! This is an easy way to save, because you are forced to save whenever you spend. If you don't want to save, don't spend!

There is another advantage to this method. Because you have to save every time you spend, you have to pay attention to your spending. Paying attention to spending can make you aware of unnecessary and mechanical spending.

Each week you should deposit all the money you saved using the "Plus Ten" method into a separate savings account.

3. Day's Due technique

Decide on an amount that you can comfortably save each day. Although in this book I suggest a minimum of $5 a day, if you can start with only $3 a day — even $1 a day — start with that amount. Consistency is important. You have to save everyday — Saturdays, Sundays, holidays — no exceptions.

What is the ideal amount to save everyday? As I said, it depends on your personal situation. You can start with $5 a day or even $1 a day. But the ideal minimum amount you should save is:

Your Annual Salary / 3,500

For example, if your annual salary is $35,000, you should aim to save: $35,000/3,500 = $10 a day.

If your annual salary is $70,000, you should aim to save $20 a day. To begin with, it does not matter what the exact amount is. But once you decide on an amount, make sure that you save that amount each day.

No matter which of the three methods you use, make sure that your savings are deposited in a separate savings account until it is time to invest. This money should not be used for any other purpose — not even in an emergency. It has been repeatedly observed that when we use this money for an emergency, soon another emergency will arise and then another emergency and then another emergency. Besides, how are we going to replace the money once we take it out? Make sure that the money you need for holidays, emergencies, and other contingencies is kept separate from your investment account.

c. AIM TO SAVE AT LEAST 10% OF YOUR INCOME

Each of the three methods described in the previous section will help you to save a minimum of 10% of your income. In my view, anyone who is seriously interested in becoming financially free should aim to save at least this much. While you can start with a smaller amount, if your savings fall below 10%, it will take you longer to achieve financial independence.

Some people may feel that they cannot possibly save 10% of their income. They should ask themselves the following question: If you cannot live on 90% of your income today, how will you get by when you retire, when your income is likely to be just one-half or one-third of your current income?

Start with $1 a day. Or $5 a day. But always aim to save at least 10% of your income. Once you make it a habit, you won't find it hard at all.

It is very important that you *do not attempt to start with an amount that is too high. You must be absolutely certain that you can keep saving at this level.* This is your first priority. Your next priority is to increase your savings to 10% of your income or higher over a period of time, even if you cannot do it right away.

d. SIX WAYS TO RAISE ADDITIONAL MONEY FOR INVESTING

If you don't have any savings now (or even if you do) you may still raise additional money for investing. My long-time friend and best-selling author, William E. Donoghue, describes six methods in his interesting book, *Guide to Finding Money to Invest*:

1. Liberate the lemons

Perhaps you have cash in various forms that is not working for you. For example, you may have some traveler's checks and foreign currency left over from your previous holiday. You may have more money in a low interest paying account than you need right now. Consolidate all such cash.

Next, go through your house room by room. Collect every item you don't like or you have not used for several months (including your clothes). Be ruthless. Organize a garage sale and sell everything you no longer use.

2. Slash your major expenses

You can cut your payments in many ways. You can cut your insurance payments by choosing the right type of insurance that will fit your needs rather than the most expensive one available. You can cut your total mortgage payments substantially by using techniques such as prepaying part of the principal or increasing the frequency of payments. You can discontinue subscriptions to magazines you hardly ever read. In fact, if you analyze your lifestyle, you may find various ways of slashing your major expenses.

3. Squeeze your budget

The trick is to squeeze your budget without getting squashed. You need to learn the art of creative scrimping. Like banking at an institution whose service charges are lower. Like buying seasonal vegetables which are likely to be fresh and less expensive than out of season produce. Don't just buy your usual choices out of habit.

4. Reduce your taxes

Or as Donoghue puts it, "reduce the thighs of your tax bill with accounting aerobics." For example, your employer may be deducting a larger than necessary amount towards taxes. Have your employer reduce your tax deduction so you have the use of your money now, rather than when you get it back from the government. Are you sure that you are claiming all the deductions you are eligible for? If not, read a good book on the subject to find out what deductions you are eligible for.

5. Increase your return without risk

Take another look at the money you have in your savings account. Can you earn a higher rate of interest at another financial institution? After all, your money is insured up to a certain amount in most institutions. As long as there is no higher risk, why not get a higher rate of return on your savings?

6. Adopt friction-free investing

Friction costs are those that you pay as commissions and loads. If you are a small investor, it is particularly important that your money supports only your investments and not someone else's lifestyle. Wherever possible, adopt friction-free investing — use discount brokers and mutual funds that charge no commission. More on this topic later.

If you cannot find any extra money even using these techniques, remember that saving $5 a day will give you $100 in three weeks' time.

7. Watch those windfalls

From time to time we all get extra money — often unexpectedly. It could be your bonus, or a tax refund or inheritance of some type, or even a small lottery winning. You should *always* save something out of every windfall. I suggest that you attempt to save at least 50% out of every windfall. If you keep adding unexpected gains to your investment program, you will reach your goal of financial freedom much sooner.

e. BUILDING AN INVESTMENT PYRAMID

All investments are not equally powerful. Some investments carry high returns and others carry low returns. Generally speaking, investments that carry high rewards tend to be risky; investments that carry low rewards tend to be less risky.

What should a small investor do? If you choose a high return investment, it is likely to carry a higher degree of risk so that you could lose a part or all of your capital. If you choose a low risk investment, your return will be low and you may have to wait a long time to become financially free.

To know what you should do, you should first list your objectives. I suggest that your objectives at this stage should be the following:

- Very important — Safety of your capital
- Important — High return
- Highly Desirable — Potentially very high return

For a conservative investor, safety of capital is of paramount importance. Why? To win the investment game, *you need to be in the game.* Once you lose your capital, you are not in the game any more. That is why preserving your capital is so important. It is so important that, to have this security, you must be willing to accept a lower rate of return at the initial stages of investing. However, as you invest more and more actively, you may want to risk a small part of your capital for a chance to win big. Sooner or later, all investors have to take some risks if they are to win big. As you start investing wisely, you will learn the difference between calculated risks and wishful thinking. Until you develop a feel for calculated risks, you should err on the cautious side.

A standard technique to achieve balance in your investments is known as the investment pyramid (see figure).

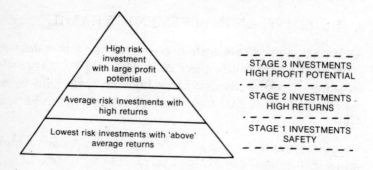

As a small investor, you need to protect your investments. Therefore, the bulk of your investments should be in low-risk, above-average return investments. This forms the base for your investment pyramid. Once the base is secure, you may want to add investments that carry average risk but above-average return. Once you have both of these types of investments, you may venture into the top of the pyramid with high-risk investments that give you an opportunity to make very high returns — if you are successful.

How much should you invest in each of the three types of investments? It depends on several factors. If you are young, you can afford to take more risks than if you are near retirement. If you are a risk-taker by nature, you may want to invest more on risky investments than if you are risk-averse by nature. A small investor is less likely to be in a position to take risks compared to a large investor.

No matter what level of risk you prefer, please remember the concept of the *pyramid*. Put more money in safe investments and less money in risky investments. This rule applies to all investors.

A broad guideline for building an investment pyramid is as follows:

- Low-risk investments: 50% to 70%

- Average-risk investments: 30% to 40%

- High-risk investments: 0% to 10%

You can change the guideline to suit your needs, but make sure that you start with a philosophy of investing. In other words, decide beforehand what is best for you. Buy only those investments that are in line with your objectives.

f. RULES OF SUCCESS FOR THE SMALL INVESTOR

The game of investing has rules. However, the rules are not the same for everyone. A small investor will have a different set of rules than a large investor. A young investor will have a different set of rules than an older investor. If you are in a high tax bracket, you will have a different set of rules than if you are in a low tax bracket. We will consider here only those rules that are useful for the small investor. Three rules are particularly useful.

1. Save regularly

If you are a small investor, you cannot afford to be irregular in your savings. Discipline is an essential part of successful investing. Once you commit yourself to save a particular amount you should stick to it. You should not make any exceptions. From time to time an unforeseen expenditure

27

may come up for which you need money. You might be tempted to skip saving that day (or month). Don't. Why? Because it has been repeatedly observed that:

If, at any time, an unexpected expenditure comes up and you fail to save because of it, another unexpected expenditure will arise in the near future. Such unexpected expenditures will keep arising over and over again until your savings program falls apart.

Therefore, small investors should make no exceptions to their savings routine. Weekends, holidays, days when you are not well — none of these should make any difference. Because you shouldn't make exceptions, you should set up a realistic program. Do not be over-ambitious and commit yourself to saving 25% of your salary, if you cannot realistically carry on the program for any length of time. Let me emphasize again: it is very important that you be consistent with your program; the amount you save is important, but not nearly as important as consistency and discipline.

2. Invest for maximum return

You might have heard — or even noticed — that the rich get richer and the poor get poorer. There is some truth to this maxim. Not only are the rich better off to begin with, they get better deals compared to the poor. Let us compare a small and a large investor:

(a) *A small investor is likely to pay a higher commission compared to a large investor.* For example, if you buy $500 worth of shares, you could be charged the maximum commission which could be 10% of your investment. A large investor who buys $10,000 worth of shares (of the same stock) will probably pay a commission of about 2%.

(b) *A small investor is likely to get a lower return compared to a large investor.* For instance, if you invest your money in Guaranteed Investment Certificates (GICs), your return will be higher if you invest a large amount, and lower if you invest a small amount. Some high-return investments (such as commercial papers) are not even open to small investors.

(c) *A small investor's investments are either vulnerable or not highly profitable.* Because small investors have fewer options compared to large investors, small investors are often forced to choose between low-return and high-risk investments.

Such a system which rewards the rich and penalizes the not-so-rich may be unfair, but it is the only system we have. It is not about to change, but take heart. This book will show how a small investor can invest *nearly as profitably as a rich investor*. There are many opportunities open to small investors. You'll find out about these opportunities in this book. If you act on these opportunities you will move into the world of high finance, no matter how little you have to invest.

3. Minimize your commissions

I have nothing against commissions. But small investors should be careful as to how they spend their capital. When you pay a large commission on an investment, you have less money to invest.

Suppose you invest $1,000 at 15% a year. If you do not have to pay any commission, you will have $4,045 at the end of ten years. On the other hand, if you have to pay a commission of 6%, you will have only $3,802 at the end of ten years. This is a difference of $243 over the investment period, one quarter of your original investment!

There is also another issue. When you pay a large commission to get into an investment, the sales person is keenly interested in selling that investment to you. It is in his or her interest to glorify the investment. I am not suggesting all sales people are unscrupulous. They are not. But it is only human nature to maximize one's personal interests. So it is up to you to look after your own interests.

Of the three requirements, you look after the first one — save regularly and I will show you how to invest for high returns and how to minimize commissions.

Now that we have finished with the preliminaries, let's go straight to discovering how you can invest to achieve financial freedom. The next part of the book describes some specific investments that are available to the small investor. Most of these investments can be bought for $100 or even less.

PART III
HOW TO INVEST:
PROFIT OPPORTUNITIES FOR THE
SMALL INVESTOR

4

GETTING STARTED

a. DOUBLE JEOPARDY

Money talks. When you have a lot of money to begin with, you can get better advice which will help you make even more money. For example, here's what you get for your money if you leave it with your bank for one year:

Amount	One year interest rate
$100	0.25%
$5,000	2.10%
$10,000	2.52%

This is what Canadian banks were paying their customers in mid-1994.

If you buy one ounce of gold bullion, you probably will pay a small premium — maybe between 3% to 6%. If you buy one gram of bullion, you will pay a minimum premium of 25%. If you buy one bond, the commission costs will be proportionately higher than if you buy ten bonds. Mutual funds that charge a commission ("load") usually reduce it for larger investors — sometimes by nearly 90%.

This is true of practically all investments.

There you have it. Double jeopardy. Small investors don't have much money to begin with *and* they have to pay out proportionately more of their money as commissions and premiums.

Besides, I'll bet if you walked into an investment company with $100,000 to invest they would take the time to sit with you and explain the options. But if you walked in with $100…

Sounds rather unfair, but that's the way it is.

b. INVESTMENTS WITH CLOUT

There is good news, however. There are investments suited to the small investor that have nearly as much clout as large investments.

Why is it that many small investors don't know much about these investments? The reason is simple. Suppose you have only $100 to invest. Even if you pay a hefty commission of 10%, your adviser receives only $10. It is simply not worth the adviser's time. The result is that small investors continue to be small — often they get even smaller.

c. TAKING RESPONSIBILITY

Let me share a secret with you. *You have all you need to succeed in investing.* I call it a secret only because so few seem to be aware of this fact. This book will support you by providing specific information. However, the final responsibility for investing is always yours. Do not invest in anything because I (or anyone else) say so. Your investment decision must make sense to you.

To be successful, you must take responsibility for your investment decisions. When you understand an investment and take responsibility for investing in it, if it fails to work out, you'll know why. You can make a better decision next time. But if you do something blindly because someone else told you so, you will learn nothing — whether your investment does well or not.

From the letters I have received from readers of earlier editions of this book, I know that thousands of people have benefited from the suggestions given. I hope the book will help you too. No matter how helpful the book is, always remember, it is your money and it is your decision.

d. A NOTE ON SPECIFIC INFORMATION

I have tried to put together all the information a small investor needs to know to invest wisely and for the highest return. I have even included the addresses and phone numbers you will need to get started.

1. Names and addresses

I have tried to exclude the names and addresses of those institutions that have an undesirable reputation. But I have no way of checking the hundreds of institutions which are listed here. Please always try to get more information before committing your money to any institution. The purpose of this book is make your search easier. You and only you are responsible for your final decision.

You should also be aware that quite often institutions move to a different address, companies merge or change their names. There is a gap between the time the book is written and the time you eventually read it. There may also be an occasional error. So if some phone numbers or addresses turn out to be incorrect, don't let that stop you. If you are serious about investing there is enough information here to get you going for the next few years!

2. Tax implications

The second thing you should be aware of is that different investment gains and losses are taxed differently. These rules can be different in the United States and Canada. Because these rules keep changing and depend on your personal situation, I do not discuss them in this book. Tax implications of your investments are important. I don't believe that they can be dealt with in a satisfactory manner in a short book on investing like this one. But that is not our concern just now. Once your program is established and you start making a sizable amount of money, you should make adjustments to your portfolio and seek the advice of a professional if necessary.

3. Canada and the United States

This book is intended for both American and Canadian investors. I refer to Canadian investments in Canadian dollars, and U.S. or international investments (including gold) in U.S. dollars.

e. HOW TO START INVESTING

Your objective is to build an investment pyramid. An investment pyramid consists of several "bricks." Each brick represents $100. If you save $5 a day, you will have $1,825 or about 18 bricks at the end of the year. Your objective is to save as many "bricks" (or units of $100) as possible each year and use them to build an investment pyramid.

Suppose you decided to save $2,100 over the next 12 months. This is equal to 21 "bricks."

First, build an imaginary pyramid of 21 bricks as shown:

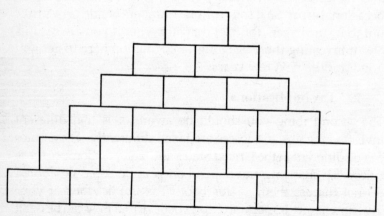

AN INVESTMENT PYRAMID WITH 21 BRICKS

Second, read through the rest of the book and decide how much you want to invest in each type of investment described. As soon as you save $100, immediately invest it according to your plan. Continue to follow your plan as you save more money. If you get some additional money unexpectedly (such as a tax refund or bonus), you may be able to build your pyramid faster than you had anticipated.

Once you have finished building one pyramid, review what you have. If you are happy with what you have, you can start building another pyramid. Repeat the procedure until you achieve financial freedom. In a later chapter I will discuss how this approach can lead you to financial freedom.

5

HOW TO GET HIGH INTEREST

Your first priority is to protect your capital and make it grow. You have started your program of saving $5 a day. After less than three weeks you will have $100. What should you do with your first $100?

You can leave it in a bank account. But this is not a very smart idea. You are unlikely to get a high interest rate. Therefore, you should seek ways of getting a higher rate of interest than you would if you just left your money in an account with your bank (or trust company, or Savings & Loan).

a. HOW LARGE INVESTORS GET HIGHER INTEREST RATES

As you might have guessed, large investors do not invest their money to get the same rate as a savings account earns. They look for much higher returns and get them.

How do large investors get a higher rate of interest? They invest in Treasury bills (T-bills). T-bills are a way of lending money to governments for a short period of time.

Or they buy Certificates of Deposit or CDs. When you buy CDs, you lend your money to banks for a fixed period.

Or they buy commercial papers. Commercial papers are a way of lending money to businesses.

The interest rate large investors earn on these investments is much higher than what they would get on a savings account in a bank — usually 2% to 5% higher. Should interest rates start moving, the interest rate on the above investments will move up immediately. The interest rate you get on a bank account may or may not move up.

Then why shouldn't we all invest in T-bills, commercial papers, and CDs? Well, there is a snag. Generally speaking, you need $5,000 to $10,000 or even more to take advantage of these opportunities. There is no way a small investor could accumulate such a large amount — at least for a few years. However, there is a way to participate in these investments with only a small amount of money. But one needs to know how.

b. HOW TO GET HIGH INTEREST RATES

To get high interest rates, you may want to join a *money market mutual fund*. What is a money market mutual fund? A money market fund is a pool of money collected from many investors — large and small — and invested in high-yielding T-bills, CDs, and commercial papers. Some of these funds will let you invest $100 or even less! Your small investment will earn an interest rate that is normally available only to large investors.

There are several advantages to investing in money market funds:

- The interest rates are higher (compared to banks, trust companies, or S&Ls)

- Interest rates are compounded daily

- Most funds charge no commission to join

- There is no penalty for withdrawal — at any time

- You can obtain your cash on any working day

- Some funds — especially in the United States — even let you write checks on your account.

c. HOW TO JOIN A MONEY MARKET FUND

Joining a money market fund is very simple. Just call or write to a money market fund and ask them to send you the details. The information package they send will contain all you need to know to open an account. Pay particular attention to:

- Minimum investment requirement

- Management fee

- Whether they charge a commission (load) to join

- Recent performance

At this stage, you should probably avoid funds that charge a commission to join. Make sure their current return is higher than what you are currently getting on your savings account.

d. NO-LOAD MUTUAL FUNDS

Throughout this book you will hear a lot about "no-load mutual funds." As explained earlier, a mutual fund collects money from a number of small and large investors and invests it on behalf of the investors. Some of these funds charge a commission that is paid out to the salespeople. Such funds are called "load" funds. Other funds do not have salespeople; they sell the fund units directly to the public. Because they do not have salespeople, they do not charge a commission to invest with them. Such funds are called "no-load funds." Whenever possible, small investors should buy "no-load" funds, thereby avoiding commission costs. Most of the funds mentioned in this book are "no-load."

e. U.S. MONEY MARKET FUNDS

There are literally hundreds of money market funds in the United States. Mutual fund companies as well as several financial institutions offer money market funds. Here are some money market funds based in the United States:

- Benham CA Tax-Free
- CMA Municipal Money Fund
- Dreyfus Municipal MMF
- Franklin Money Market Fund
- INVESCO Money Market Fund
- Mariner Tax-Free MMF
- Rodney Square: Money Market Portfolio
- Scudder Managed Tax-Free Fund
- USAA Money Market Fund

f. CANADIAN MONEY MARKET FUNDS

In Canada, there are over 100 money market funds. Most of them are new. A majority of these funds require an initial investment of at least $1,000 or more. Some funds will accept $500. The funds listed below require only a $100 minimum. Once you join the fund, they may even accept a lower amount when you add to your initial investment. None of these funds charge a commission to join.

- CDA RSP Money Market Fund
- Great West Life Money Market Inv. Fund
- Montreal Trust: Money Market Section (10 Units)
- Montreal Trust RRSP/RRIF: Montreal Market (10 Units)

For more details of all funds listed in this chapter, please refer to the Resource Directory at the end.

g. WHEN TO USE MONEY MARKET FUNDS

Money market funds will give you a better rate of return compared to a savings account. But putting your money in a money market fund is not the best way to get rich. This is because the interest you receive through money market funds is fully taxed. Unless the interest rates are high (as, for example, they were during most of the 1980s), taxes and inflation will cancel out most of your gains. Some of your money can be in money market funds. However, the main use of money market funds is to park your money when you have not yet decided what to do with it.

h. HOW TO EVALUATE THE PERFORMANCE OF YOUR FUND

Before you start investing, you may want to compare the performance of different funds. You may also want to monitor how your fund is doing. Part V, Keeping Track of Your Progress, will show you how.

6

HOW TO INVEST IN STOCKS

Perhaps you have never invested in the stock market. Maybe you wonder what the stock market is, and wonder how you can make money investing in stocks. Even if you are an absolute beginner, you will find this chapter helpful.

a. WHAT ARE SHARES?

Shares indicate ownership of a corporation. If a corporation issues 100,000 shares and if you buy 1,000 of these, you own 1% of the company.

Corporations issue shares to raise money. Let us assume that you have a great idea for manufacturing widgets that will generate large profits. But you need start-up capital of $1 million. So you start a corporation and issue 200,000 shares at $10 each. You keep 100,000 shares or 50% of the company for yourself and sell the remaining 100,000 shares at $10 each. This gives you the $1 million you need to manufacture widgets.

Once these shares are issued, investors who bought these shares will not normally be able to sell them back to the corporation. But they can sell them to other investors. The price of these shares on any given day is determined by market forces — supply and demand. If there are more buyers than sellers, the price will go up; if there are more sellers than buyers, the price will come down. If the corporation makes large profits, the price of the shares will go up. If it makes large losses, the price will come down.

Within a single day the price may go up or down several times, depending on supply and demand for that stock on that day.

b. HOW ARE SHARES TRADED?

Generally, stocks are bought and sold from a few central locations called stock exchanges (such as the New York Stock Exchange and the Toronto Stock Exchange). Shares are traded at the exchanges through auction.

c. HOW TO BUY AND SELL SHARES

If you want to buy or sell shares, you need to go through a stockbroker who will arrange for the transaction to take place. The normal procedure is to simply call your broker on the telephone and place an order to buy or sell a certain number of shares of a stock.

d. HOW TO FIND A STOCKBROKER

There are two kinds of stockbrokers: Full service and discount. *Full service brokers* charge a higher commission, but they are likely to provide the information you need about your stock. They also make recommendations regarding what stock to buy. A good full service stockbroker will try to understand your objectives, how much risk you want to take with your money, and whether a given investment is suitable for you or not. *Discount brokers,* on the other hand, simply take your order and execute it. Because they don't provide any additional service, their commission charges are lower.

Many people choose brokers by "word-of-mouth" — on the recommendation of friends and acquaintances. The other way to choose a broker is to look through the Yellow Pages of your phone book and pick a firm that is a member in all major exchanges. Call the firm and ask to talk to a broker. You will be put in touch with the "broker of the day." He or she will probably arrange to have a personal meeting with you and take down all the required information to open an account. Once the account is opened, you can carry out all the transactions over the telephone.

e. HOW TO PLACE ORDERS WITH YOUR BROKER

Once you decide what stock to buy, you can simply call your broker to buy "100 shares of XYZ company at $ ___ per share." If you do not specify a price that you are willing to pay, your broker will buy shares *at the market price* (the price at which the stock is available when your order reaches the stock exchange).

If you specify a price at which the stock should be bought, you have placed what is known as a GTC (Good Till Canceled) order. A GTC order will remain with the broker until the order is executed or you cancel the order. Suppose XYZ stock is trading at $10.25 and you do not want to pay more than $10 for it. You may place an order to buy 100 shares of XYZ at $10. Your order will be active for about 30 days. During this time, if XYZ sells for $10, it will be bought at that price for you.

f. WHAT ELSE SHOULD YOU KNOW?

Stocks are usually sold in multiples of 100. One hundred shares are called a *board lot* or a *round lot*. You can of course buy less than 100 shares. When you buy less than 100 shares, you are said to be dealing in *odd lots*. However, commission charges are higher for odd lots.

The price of a stock *usually* goes up or down by a minimum of one-eighth of a dollar, e.g., $7\frac{1}{8}$, $7\frac{1}{4}$, $7\frac{3}{8}$, etc. Lower priced stocks go up and down in steps of one-sixteenth or one thirty-second of a dollar. Penny stocks (very low-priced stocks) go up or down in steps of one cent.

g. WHAT ARE OTC STOCKS?

Some stocks are not traded through stock exchanges. Instead, they are traded through an electronic network of dealers. The stocks traded this way are called OTC (over-the-counter) stocks. While there may be exciting opportunities in this sector of the market, you should be aware of certain disadvantages:

- Less information is readily available about OTC stocks.

- You may find that few newspapers carry complete listings of these stocks. Every time you want to know the price at which these stocks trading, you have to call your broker.

h. HOW TO READ THE FINANCIAL PAGE

Each day, major newspapers list the stocks that are traded in the main stock exchanges. They are usually listed as follows:

12 Month				PE				
High	Low	Stock	Volume	Ratio	High	Low	Close	Change
16	12	NSF Bank	20,000	20	15	13	14½	-½

The third column (Stock) indicates the name of the company whose stocks are under consideration. The first two columns (12 Month High-Low) indicates that in the past 12 months, NSF Bank shares were sold as high as $16 a share, and as low as $12 a share. The Volume column indicates how many shares changed hands during the day. PE ratio (price earnings ratio) is explained in section j. below. In general, the lower the PE ratio, the better it is from an investment point of view.

The next three columns summarize the previous day's transactions: the stock sold for as high as $15 and as low as $13, and the last trade occurred at $14½. The last column shows the difference between yesterday's closing and the previous day's closing. In the example, yesterday's closing

46

price was $14\frac{1}{2}$. The change is $\frac{1}{2}$, that is, the previous day's closing price was $15.

i. WHAT IS A STOP-LOSS ORDER?

Suppose you buy a stock at $10, hoping that it will increase in value. Since you can never be certain of this, you may want to limit your losses should the price fall. You may decide to take a loss of 15%, but not much more. In this case, you may enter a stop-loss order with your broker at $8.50. If the price of the stock reaches $8.50, your broker will automatically sell your shares at the best possible price available at that time.

j. HOW TO MINIMIZE THE RISK

The stock you buy can either go up or go down. Although we all hope that the stocks we buy will go up, there is no guarantee. To minimize the risk of losing money on a stock, you may want to follow these guidelines.

1. Buy stocks with low price earnings (PE) ratio

Suppose a share costs $10 and the company earns $2 per share. That is, the company makes $2 for each $10 you invest. The price earnings is simply

$$\text{PE Ratio} = \frac{\text{Price Per Share}}{\text{Earnings Per Share}} = \frac{\$10}{\$2} = 5$$

The higher the earnings, the lower the PE ratio. Therefore, if the PE ratio is low, say six or lower, the price of the stock is less likely to go down compared to another stock with a much higher PE ratio (all things being equal). Financial pages report the PE ratios of most major stocks daily.

2. Buy stocks with high book values

Book value tells us how much a company is worth. For example, if a company had net assets of $100 million with 10 million shares outstanding, its book value is $100 million divided by 10 million = $10 per share.

If the company ceased to operate, each share would still be worth $10. Therefore, it is safer to buy stocks that trade close to and lower than their book value. Book values are not usually reported in the financial pages of the newspapers. Perhaps the simplest way to find out the book value of any given stock is to ask your broker.

k. COMMISSIONS: HOW TO REDUCE THEM

Whenever you buy or sell shares, you have to pay a commission to the broker. This could be as high as 3% when you buy, and 3% when you sell. Many brokerage houses have a minimum commission of $40 to $60. In return for this commission, a full-service brokerage house will provide research information and advice on stocks.

However, many small investors may find the commission costs rather high. If you are sure of what you want to buy, then you can save on commissions by going to discount brokerage houses. Discount brokerage houses generally will not offer you any advice. They will simply execute your orders.

If you want to use a discount broker, make sure that the discounts offered are meaningful. If you write to them, they will send you a schedule of their charges for different transactions. You can then compare and decide.

Many discount brokers advertise their services in newspapers such as the *Wall Street Journal*, the *New York Times* (for the United States) or the *Globe and Mail Report on Business* (for Canada).

Here is a partial list of some discount brokers in the United States and Canada. (For full addresses and telephone numbers, see the Resources Directory at the end of this book.)

United States

- Bidwell
- Burke Christensen & Lewis

- Fidelity Brokerage Services Inc.
- Heartland Securities
- Lombard Institutional Brokerage
- National Discount Brokers
- Pacific Brokerage Services
- Quick and Reilly Inc.
- Charles Schwab and Co.
- Muriel Siebert and Co.
- York Securities

Canada

- Toronto Dominion Greenline 1-800-268-8209
- Bank of Montreal Investor Services (416) 867-4000
- Desjardins Securities 1-800-268-8471
- Scotia Discount Brokerage (416) 863-7411

1. WHY DIRECT INVESTMENT MAY NOT BE SUITABLE FOR THE SMALL INVESTOR

Although I have discussed stock market investments at considerable length, direct stock market investments may not be suitable for the small investor for the following reasons:

(a) Individual stock can be *expensive*. For example, in early 1994, Microsoft shares were selling at $96.50 per share. To buy 100 shares, an investor would need as much as $9,650.

(b) The *commission* can be high. For example, for the above transaction you may have to pay more than $290 in commission charges. When you sell you may have to pay another $290.

(c) You *cannot spread the risk*. Even after spending $10,230, you hold only one stock, you are totally dependent on this company thriving for you to make money.

Obviously, it would be preferable for the small investor to find a stock market investment medium that is less expensive, involves little commission, and is less risky.

Is there such a medium?

Yes, there is! In fact, you can start with as low as $100, pay no commission, and spread the risk.

m. HOW YOU CAN PARTICIPATE IN THE STOCK MARKET

The investment medium I am talking about is *mutual funds.* As mentioned earlier, a mutual fund is an investment company whose main purpose is the investment and management of investors' money. When you invest your money in a mutual fund, it is pooled with that of other investors and is invested in a wide variety of stocks. This minimizes your cost as well as your risk.

Some mutual funds charge a commission; others do not. Those that do not charge a commission are called *no-load mutual* funds. There is no evidence to show that funds that charge a commission perform better than those that do not. Hence, a new investor is better off investing in a no-load fund.

No-load mutual funds have the following advantages:

- *No sales commissions.*

- *No high-pressure salespeople:* No-load funds have no salespeople; that's the reason you do not pay any commission.

- *Greater safety:* Since the fund invests in a variety of companies, the investment is diversified. This usually minimizes your risk.

- *Ease of operation:* Obviously it is easier to buy and sell a single fund than a wide variety of stocks. Some funds allow you to buy and sell over the telephone.

- *Variety:* There are several types of funds. There are funds that specialize in high dividend yielding stocks (income funds); funds that invest in stocks that are likely to appreciate greatly in value (growth stocks); funds that invest in stocks that relate to natural resources; funds that invest in foreign securities (international funds); funds that invest in bonds (bond funds) and so on. Depending on your requirements, you can choose a fund that is right for you.

Given all these advantages, the no-load mutual fund is perhaps the best way for a beginner to get started in the stock market.

For further information on selecting a mutual fund, you can obtain the *Investment Company Institute's Guide to Mutual Funds.* It costs $8.50. The 1994 edition of this guide contains information on over 3,000 U.S. mutual funds.

The Investment Company Institute
1401 H Street N.W.
Washington, DC 20005
(202) 326-5800

For an extensive list of no-load or low-load mutual funds (including the minimum required and the nature of each fund), you may want to consult *Investor's Guide to Low-Cost Mutual Funds.* It is published by the Mutual Fund Education Alliance and costs $5. The guide has detailed information on 750 funds, including their one-, five-, and ten-year performances.

Mutual Fund Education Alliance
1900 Erie Street, Suite 120
Kansas City, MO 64116
(816) 471-1454

If you are a small investor, the following no-load mutual funds may be suitable for you since *no minimum* amount is required to join.

United States

- Twentieth Century Growth

- Twentieth Century Select

- Twentieth Century Heritage

- Twentieth Century International Equity

- Twentieth Century Long Term Bond

- Twentieth Century Ultra

- Twentieth Century Vista

- Beacon Hill Mutual Fund

(The addresses and phone numbers for the above funds are in the Resource Directory.)

Canada

Of late, no-load funds have been gaining in popularity in Canada. Consequently there are many more no-load mutual funds today than there were about ten years ago. Most funds, however, require a minimum — usually between $100 and $1,000. Here are some funds that require $150 or less to join:

- Associate Investors Limited

- Great West Life Equity Index

- Foresters Growth Fund ($50 minimum)

- RoyFund Equity Ltd. ($100 minimum)

- Montreal Trust Excelsior Funds: Equity Fund

If you need additional information, contact:

The Investment Fund Institute of Canada
151 Yonge Street, Suite 503
Toronto, Ontario
M5C 2W7
(416) 363-2158

Ask for their membership list. The list gives the addresses and phone numbers of several mutual funds. Examine the performance of these funds with other funds as well. Performance of all Canadian funds are published monthly by the *Financial Post*, the *Globe and Mail Report on Business*, and the *Financial Times of Canada* monthly survey. (The *Financial Times of Canada*, for example, compares the performance of several Canadian funds on ten-year, five-year, three-year, one-year, and quarterly and monthly bases. This survey is usually published in the third week of every month). Contact those funds that have performed well over the years to find out their terms and conditions.

n. HOW TO CHOOSE A FUND

Choosing a fund among the several that are available depends on several factors.

(a) *The amount of money you have:* Different funds have different minimum investment requirements. You are obviously restricted by the amount of money you have to invest.

(b) *Your investment needs:* As mentioned earlier, different funds are geared to different needs. For example, if you want high current yield, an income fund is a better choice. If you are not interested in high current income but would rather invest in stocks that are likely to increase substantially in value, you would choose a growth fund. Or you may prefer to invest in different types of funds as money becomes available to you.

(c) *Funds' past performance:* A fund that has done consistently well in the past is likely to do well in the future. The performance of a fund should be judged over a period of time (at least the five previous years) and not just on the past 12 months. Any fund can do well or badly in a given year. Consistently good performance, on the other hand, seldom happens by chance.

To give you sufficient flexibility, I have listed a wide variety of funds in the United States and in Canada in the Resource Directory at the end of this book. Before subscribing to any of the funds, obtain prospectuses from different funds and compare their differences and long-term performances.

7

HOW TO BUY STOCKS AT A DISCOUNT

When you go to a discount broker, you pay a lower commission. But there is a way to avoid commissions completely. In fact, you can even buy stocks at a discount! This may sound too good to be true, but you can do it by taking advantage of a less-widely known program called DRIPs.

a. DIVIDEND REINVESTMENT INVESTMENT PLANS (DRIPs)

DRIPs stands for "Dividend Reinvestment Investment Plans." As you know, many stocks pay regular dividends. Some stocks that pay regular dividends have set up DRIPs that let you reinvest your dividends without commissions.

All you have to do to join the DRIP program of a given stock is own just one share in the company. Once you buy the share, you should register the stock in your name. The transfer agent for the company will send you the necessary forms. Indicate that you want to be in the DRIP program. You will then receive all the necessary details.

b. THE ADVANTAGES OF JOINING A DRIP

DRIPs offer you an opportunity to reinvest the dividends you receive in additional stocks automatically. In most cases, no commission is involved. Many companies will let you buy additional shares, and others will let you buy shares at a 5% discount.

If you add this 5% discount to the 2% commission which you would normally pay, you see that you pay $100 for what would cost most people $107. A 7% return on your investment before you even start is not a bad deal!

Dividend paying companies tend to be established, stable companies. Therefore, we have a degree of safety built in when we join the DRIP program offered by a company.

Here are the advantages of joining a DRIP program:

- Your dividends are automatically reinvested.

- You may be allowed to buy more shares with no commission.

- In some cases, you may buy shares at a discount.

- Your investment is relatively safe.

c. INFORMATION ON DRIP COMPANIES

You can obtain information on companies that participate in the DRIP program from stock exchanges.

United States

In the United States, there are also newsletters that specialize in DRIP investing. An example of such a newsletter would be:

DRIP Investor
7412 Calumet Avenue
Hammond, IN 46324-2692

Canada

For example, in Canada, the Toronto Stock Exchange provides a listing of DRIP companies along with the terms and conditions. This can be purchased for about $12. (For the addresses of the Toronto and other stock exchanges, see the Resource Directory at the end of the book.) If you are interested in DRIPs, you should contact stock exchanges for more details.

d. HOW TO JOIN A DRIP

If you are interested in a DRIP program this is what you should do.

(a) Get a list of companies that offer a DRIP program by contacting the stock exchanges.

(b) Go through the list by choosing those companies that seem attractive to you.

(c) Of these companies, see which ones have more favorable terms.

(d) Buy some stocks in each company you are interested in by going through a stockbroker. (There also other methods: you can buy DRIP stock in some financial trade shows or through some organizations. These methods are beyond the scope of this book.)

(e) Get the forms from the "transfer agent" for the company.

(f) Fill out the form indicating that you would like to be in the DRIP program.

(g) Once you have done this, you will automatically receive information which will enable you take advantage of the DRIP program.

e. WHAT ELSE SHOULD YOU KNOW?

While DRIP investing is attractive, please bear in mind that only a handful of companies offer this program. Many companies that are attractive from an investment point of view may not offer a DRIP program. You should definitely consider a DRIP program, but you should also consider that avoiding commissions and buying a stock at a discount is only one aspect of investing. The real meat of investing is in making your money grow. If you find a stock that makes your money grow faster, don't let go of the opportunity just because it does not offer a DRIP program.

8
HOW TO INVEST IN BONDS

a. WHAT ARE BONDS?

Governments and corporations need to borrow money from time to time. To do this, they issue bonds to the public. Thus, when you buy a bond, you are lending your money to the government or to the corporation for a specified period of time. In return for this, you are paid regular interest.

Every bond has three features:

(a) A *face value* or the loan amount (usually $1,000).

(b) A specified *rate of interest* (called the *coupon* rate).

(c) A *maturity date*. (This is the date on which the company or government will buy the bond back from you at the face value.)

Suppose you buy a bond that matures after ten years. What happens if you need the money after five years? The company or the government will not normally buy it back from you until the maturity (or redemption) date. However, you can sell it to some other investor in the bond market. When you sell your bond to another investor in the open market, the price you get will depend on supply and demand factors. You may get less than what you paid for it or you may get more.

b. BOND PRICES

What determines how much you will get for your bond before the maturity date? It depends on interest rates. If interest rates are higher when you want to sell than when you

58

bought the bonds, you will get a lower price for your bonds. If the interest rates are lower when you want to sell than when you bought the bonds, you will get a higher price for your bonds. In short, when interest rates go up, the prices come down; when the interest rates come down, the prices go up.

Suppose you buy a bond for $1,000 and the interest rate is 10%. If the interest rate paid by financial institutions such as banks, moves up to 12% then investors will not be willing to pay $1,000 for your bond, because your bond pays only 10% interest and they can get 12% buying newly issued bonds. But if you sell your bonds at a discount, say for $850, investors will buy it from you. When this happens, your bonds are said to be "trading at a discount." Although you sold your bond at $850, when the maturity date arrives, the person holding the bond will get the full $1,000. The difference between what you got ($1,000) and what you paid ($850) is known as "capital gains." Capital gains are taxed at a lower rate in the United States and in Canada.

On the other hand, suppose you buy a bond for $1,000 and the interest rate is 10%. If the interest rate moves down to 8%, then investors may be willing to pay more than $1,000 for your bond, because new bonds pay only 8% interest while yours pays 10%. You may be able to sell your bond, for example, for $1,150. When this happens, your bonds are said to be *trading at a premium*. Although you sold your bond at $1,150, when the maturity date arrives, the person holding the bond will get only $1,000.

c. WHEN TO BUY BONDS

Because the value of bonds goes up when the interest rate goes down, *you should buy bonds when you expect the interest rate to go down*. When the price of the bond you bought goes up and you sell, you make a profit and this profit will be treated as capital gains. Capital gains usually get better tax treatment in the United States and Canada. You should be careful when buying a bond that trades at a premium. Unless the interest rate comes down before the maturity date, you will get back less than the amount you paid for it.

d. BONDS AND DEBENTURES

Bonds are generally issued with collateral. The company issuing a bond backs it up with specific assets. Debentures, on the other hand, are issued without any collateral. You buy debentures based on the reputation of the company issuing it. All government "bonds" are really debentures — you cannot force the government to sell off the parliament building to repay your bond. How do you know how safe your bond is? There are independent bond rating services that rate all bonds. Your broker should be able to tell you the rating of any major bond. Safer bonds tend to have slightly lower interest rates compared to bonds that are less safe.

e. HOW TO BUY

Bonds can be bought and sold through a stockbroker. The commission costs for bonds are much lower than for stocks.

f. BOND AND MORTGAGE FUNDS

Since most bonds cost around $1,000, a small investor may not be able to diversify properly. Besides, many investors may not want to be bothered about selecting suitable bonds for their portfolios. *Bond funds* overcome these problems by pooling the money received from many investors and investing it in a portfolio of bonds, mortgages, or both. Interest rates influence bond funds in the same way that interest rates influence bonds.

The following bond funds require $100 or less to join (for addresses and phone numbers see the Resource Directory):

United States

- Franklin Short-Intermediate U.S. Government Securities ($100 minimum)
- Twentieth Century Long-Term Bond (No minimum)

Canada

- Barreau du Quebec Fonds Placement — Obligations (No minimum)
- RoyFund Bond Fund ($100 minimum)
- Montreal Trust Excelsior Funds: Income Fund

There are over 125 bond and mortgage funds in Canada. There are even more in the United States. See the Resource Directory for a listing of some of these funds.

g. STRIPS AND ZEROS

Stripped bonds are like any other bearer bond in that they are issued with coupons attached to them so bond holders can exchange the "coupons" for interest payments. To "strip" a bond, an investment dealer buys a block of these bonds and removes all the coupons. The bond is then called the "residue." You can buy either the "coupon" part or the "residue" part. If you buy the coupon part, you get the regular interest rate, but you will not benefit if the price of the bond goes up.

If you buy the residue part, you will get no interest at all, but you will pay a much lower price to buy the bond. For instance, if you can find a strip bond that matures in 25 years with a 12% coupon, you need to invest only $5,825 today to receive $100,000 at the end of the term. Strip bonds also rise sharply when the interest rate goes down.

Zero coupon bonds are similar to stripped bonds in that you can buy a $1,000 bond for a fraction of its face value. You will not be paid any interest, but when the bond matures you will be able to redeem it for its full face value.

The main attraction of these bonds is that they enable you to lock in at a high yield for a long time. This is particularly advantageous if interest rates go down in the future. On the other hand, if interest rates go up, you will be locked into a lower yield. If you want to sell your bond at that time, you will get a much lower price than you paid for it. Even small fluctuations in interest rates will make the market price of these bonds go up and down.

One main disadvantage of these strips in Canada is that you are expected to pay taxes regularly even though you do not receive any interest. The interest is deemed to have been received by you on a regular basis for tax purposes. (Canadian investors may buy stripped bonds for their RRSPs where it is not taxed until the plan is closed).

You can use strips and zeros to your advantage by buying a few bonds each year with different maturity dates. These may be used to supplement your income in later years.

There are also mutual funds that invest in zero coupon bonds. (These funds are U.S.-based). You may want to consider the following zero coupon funds:

- Benham Target Maturities Trust series 2000

- Benham Target Maturities Trust series 2005

- Benham Target Maturities Trust series 2010

- Benham Target Maturities Trust series 2015

- Benham Target Maturities Trust series 2020

All these funds are no-load and require a minimum investment of $1,000. To get the prospectus for any or all of these funds please contact:

Benham Management Corp.
1665 Charleston Road
Mountain View, CA 94043
1-800-321-8321 / (415) 965-4222

h. CONVERTIBLE BONDS

Convertible bonds are like any other bond except for one special feature: they give you the privilege of exchanging the bonds for a specified number of shares of the company before a certain date. Because of this attractive feature, the interest rate is usually lower.

For example, Labatts has a convertible bond which pays a fixed interest rate of 5%. You can also exchange this bond for 37 shares of Labatts. Labatts was trading at $21 (in early May, 1994). Suppose the price of these shares moves up to $25. Since you can convert your bond into 37 shares, it will now be worth at least $925 (37 x $25). In fact it will be worth more because the bond pays interest as well. Thus, when share prices rise, convertible bonds automatically benefit.

On the other hand, suppose the stock goes down to $15 per share. Then the share value of your bond will be only $555 (37 x $15). But the price of the bond will not decline that much because, unlike the shares, convertible bonds pay interest. Thus, when share prices decline, convertible bonds will not decline to the same extent.

In other words, when the share prices increase, convertible bonds behave like shares with unlimited profit potential. When share prices go down, convertible bonds are partially protected against corresponding declines because of their interest yielding feature.

1. What to look for in convertible bonds

The convertible feature is of no great benefit if the total value of the share per bond is too low relative to the cost of the bond. This would mean that the shares have to move up significantly before you can make a profit. Therefore, when you buy a convertible bond, you should make sure that the premium is not too high. (Higher premiums will be asked for when the underlying stock is expected to move up and when the bond has a high coupon.) Premium is calculated as follows:

Percent premium =
$$\frac{[(100 \times \text{Current bond price})]}{(\text{No. of shares per bond} \times \text{Current stock price})]} - 100$$

You also have to look for the actual rate of interest. This is calculated as follows:

Percent current interest = (100 x Interest specified on the bond) ÷ Current bond price

You should look for convertible bonds with low premiums and high current yield. Bonds trading close to (or below) their par value are more desirable than bonds that trade at a price that is much higher.

2. When to buy convertible bonds

A convertible bond is a good buy when —

- the current interest on the bond is not too low compared to regular bonds,

- the conversion is relatively low (under 20%),

- there are reasons to believe that the underlying stock will rise,

- interest rates are falling, but the stock is rising, and

- the bond is not trading above its par value (usually $1,000).

The last feature is particularly important because many convertible bonds have a "call feature" which gives the corporation the right to buy the bond back at a specified price on or after a specified date. Once a bond is called, you will get only the specified price, no matter how much you paid to get it.

You have to be careful when —

- the bond is selling much above its face value,
- the conversion premium is high but the current yield is low,
- the call features are due soon,
- the interest rates are rising but the share prices are falling,
- the share price is not likely to go up, and
- the underlying company is not sound.

There are not many convertible bond funds in Canada. Even in the United States there are only a few. These funds either charge a commission or have lackluster performance, or both.

Convertible bonds can be very profitable, provided you choose the right ones at the right time. You might be better off investing directly in them (if you find good convertible bonds) rather than through a mutual fund.

3. How is the gain taxed?

The interest paid on the bond is fully taxed as interest income. If the bond goes up in price and you sell it, the profit will be treated as capital gains and taxed (or not taxed) accordingly.

9
HOW TO INVEST IN PREFERRED STOCKS

a. WHAT IS A PREFERRED STOCK?

A preferred stock, like a common stock, represents shares of ownership in a company. A preferred stock carries a fixed rate of dividend. This dividend must be paid before any dividend on common stocks. However, preferred shares do not carry voting rights.

Although a preferred stock technically represents ownership, it works like a bond. There are some differences:

- Bonds pay an indicated rate of interest while preferred stocks pay an indicated rate of dividend.

- In general, the interest you receive from bonds is fully taxed (there are some exceptions to this rule), while dividends received on preferred stocks will be taxed at a favorable rate.

- Bonds in general have a maturity date, the day on which you will receive the face value of the bond; preferred shares do not have maturity dates.

- Most bonds have a face value of $1,000. Interest is calculated on this face value, no matter what price you paid to buy the bond. Most preferred shares have a face value of $25.

b. WHY INVEST IN A PREFERRED STOCK?

In spite of their differences, both bonds and preferred shares are bought for steady income. Preferred stocks are bought for exactly the same reasons as bonds. Whether you buy bonds or preferred stocks depends on your tax situation and the level of security you want with your income.

c. DIFFERENT KINDS OF PREFERRED STOCKS

Some corporations issue Class A preferred shares, Class B preferred shares, and so on. In such cases, Class A share dividends must be paid prior to Class B share dividends, Class B before Class C, and so on. Class A preferred shares would then be called *prior preferred*.

Certain types of preferred shares are known as *participating preferreds*. Holders of these preferreds are entitled to additional dividends if the common stock dividends exceed a certain amount.

Cumulative preferreds guarantee that the accumulated dividend will be paid later if it cannot be paid when it is due. Such payments will take precedence over common stock dividends.

Convertible preferreds are similar to convertible bonds in that they can be exchanged for a specified number of common shares at the holder's option. This feature is attractive if the common stock is on its way up.

Retractable preferreds give the holder the right to redeem his or her shares after a specific date at a specific price. This feature may be useful should the value of the preferred stock decline.

Except in the case of convertible preferreds, preferred shares are generally bought for high current yields. Preferred shares do not have the same potential for appreciation, except when interest rates are on the decline. Newer issues, however, have some innovative features (like variable interest rates) that make them attractive as a conservative investment medium. You should look into these features before you invest.

d. PREFERRED STOCK PRICES

Once issued to the public, preferred stock trades on stock exchanges. The price of a preferred stock will depend on prevailing interest rates. If the interest rates are higher when you want to sell than when you bought the preferred stock, you will get a lower price than what you paid for it. If the interest rates are lower when you want to sell than when you bought the preferred stock, you will get a higher price for your preferred stock. In short, when the interest rates go up, the prices come down; when the interest rates come down, the prices go up. Preferred share prices go up and down with interest rates, but in the opposite direction. This is exactly how bonds behave as well.

e. WHEN TO BUY PREFERRED STOCKS

Because the value of preferred stocks goes up when the interest rate goes down, you should buy preferred stocks when you expect the interest rate to go down. When the price of the preferred stock you bought goes up and you sell, you make a profit and this profit will be treated as capital gains. Capital gains usually get better tax treatment in the United States and Canada.

f. HOW TO BUY/SELL PREFERRED STOCKS

Because preferred shares trade on stock exchanges, you would buy preferred shares in the same way you would buy bonds: through your stockbroker.

g. USING MUTUAL FUNDS TO BUY PREFERRED STOCKS

There are mutual funds that specialize in dividend income. Most of these mutual funds are heavily invested in preferred stocks. (They also invest in dividend-paying common stocks.) Here are some no-load, dividend-income mutual funds:

United States

In the United States, mutual funds are not generally identified as preferred income funds. If you are interested in dividend oriented stocks, you should look under the category "Growth and Income Funds." I recommend that you consult *Low-Load Mutual Funds* published each year by the American Association of Individual Investors.

Canada

- Montreal Trust Excelsior Funds: Dividend Fund
- National Trust Dividend Fund ($500 minimum)
- Royfund Dividend Fund ($100 minimum)
- Royal Trust Growth & Income Fund ($500 minimum)

10

HOW TO INVEST INTERNATIONALLY

a. WHY INVEST ABROAD?

Many investors think that only the rich should invest in foreign countries. But there is money to be made in foreign countries, and foreign investing is not difficult. You do not need a lot of money either.

Between October 1, 1992, and September 30, 1993, the U.S. stock market gained 11% and the Canadian stock market gained just 4%. For the same period, the Singapore stock market gained 59%, the Malaysian stock market gained 57%, the New Zealand stock market gained 49%, the Italian stock market gained 44%, and the Japanese stock market gained 41%.

Why shouldn't you have a piece of the action? Different countries grow at different rates. By investing only in Canada or in the United States, you can miss the growth that is taking place elsewhere. The world is becoming smaller and smaller. If you arbitrarily decide to invest in only one country, it is unlikely that you will do as well as you would if you invested abroad. If you had started with about $500 in 1960 and shifted the money into different markets at the right time, you would have well over $1 million by now! (See Chart #2.) Yet, you would have moved your money only 16 times in 25 years!

Since the chart was produced about five years ago, you could have increased your investment by another 50% (another $500,000) by simply moving your investments three more times!

CHART #2
INTERNATIONAL INVESTMENTS
Turning $500 into $1,000,000

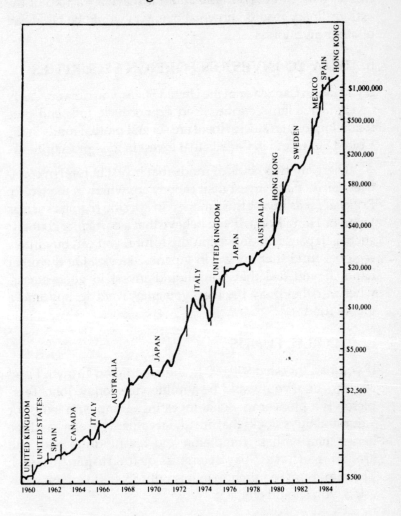

Concept and data: International Bank Credit Analyst and Capital International Perspective (brought to the author's attention by Adrian Day).

I am not suggesting that you could have predicted precisely which country would do well. I don't think anybody can do that. But even if you could achieve a fraction of the extraordinary results shown above, you would be far ahead of other investors.

b. HOW TO INVEST IN FOREIGN SECURITIES

If you live in Canada or in the United States, you can very easily invest in foreign securities. You do not have to spend time following foreign stocks; there are several mutual funds in the United States and in Canada that invest in foreign securities.

There are two kinds of funds that invest in foreign countries. *Global funds* invest their money anywhere in the world. *Regional funds* invest their money in specific regions such as Japan or Hong Kong. If you believe that a particular country, such as Japan, will do well in the future, you can buy into a regional fund that invests in Japanese stocks. On the other hand, if you feel that you should invest in good stocks, wherever they may be, then you may want to buy into a global fund.

c. GLOBAL FUNDS

If you had invested $30,000 in the Templeton Growth Fund 30 years ago, you would be a millionaire today. John Templeton is a pioneer in global investing. Templeton looks for value and buys stocks that are undervalued. No one has done better than he has. Templeton and his fund are both still around. You have to pay a commission (6%) to join this fund. The minimum required to join is only $500. If you are interested, you should contact:

Templeton Growth Fund
700 Central Avenue
P.O. Box 33030
St. Petersburg, FL 33701
(813) 823-8712
1-800-237-0738 (toll-free)

In Canada, contact:

Templeton Growth Fund
4 King Street West
19th Floor
Toronto, Ontario
M5W 1N3
(416) 364-4672
1-800-387-0830 (toll-free)

Currently there are several mutual funds that invest internationally. Here are a few funds that charge no commissions. Their addresses and phone numbers can be found in the Resource Directory at the end of the book.

United States

- Harbor International Fund
- Scudder Global Fund
- Vanguard International Gr. Fund
- T. Rose International Bond Fund
- USAA International Fund

Canada

- Altamira Asia Pacific Fund
- Altamira New Asia Fund
- CIBC Global Equity Fund
- Capstone International Investment Trust
- Cornerstone Global Fund
- Everest EuroGrowth Fund
- First Canadian International Growth Fund
- Hong Kong Bank Asian Growth
- Montreal Trust Excelsior Funds: International Section
- Royal Trust Asian Growth Fund

d. REGIONAL FUNDS

If you are interested in investing in a specific country, you can do so through a closed-end fund. A closed-end fund is a company whose sole business is to invest its capital for its shareholders. Once a closed-end fund starts operating, it will not accept new money from investors. But you can buy and sell shares in a closed-end fund just like you would buy and sell the shares of any publicly traded company — on a stock exchange. Some of these funds can trade at a premium or at a discount from their net asset value. If you want to invest in any of these funds, you may want to ask your broker whether the fund is trading at a discount or at a premium. You should avoid funds that are trading at a premium, especially if the premium is large. Here a few funds that invest in different countries:

- European Investment Concept Fund (New York Stock Exchange)
- Asia Pacific Fund (New York Stock Exchange)
- Brazil Fund (New York Stock Exchange)
- Emerging Mexico Fund (New York Stock Exchange)
- First Australia Fund (American Stock Exchange)
- France Growth Fund (New York Stock Exchange)
- New Germany Fund (Toronto Stock Exchange)
- India Growth Fund (New York Stock Exchange)
- First Israel Fund (OTC)
- Italy Fund (New York Stock Exchange)
- Japan Equity Fund (Toronto Stock Exchange)
- Korea Fund (New York Stock Exchange)
- Malaysia Fund (New York Stock Exchange)
- Growth of Spain Fund (New York Stock Exchange)

- Swiss Helvetica Fund (Toronto Stock Exchange)
- Taiwan Fund (New York Stock Exchange)
- Thai Capital Fund (New York Stock Exchange)
- United Kingdom Fund (New York Stock Exchange)

e. BEFORE YOU START

If you want to invest in foreign securities, I suggest that you write to different funds and compare their track records before investing. You may also want to read a good book on international investing. There are several books on the market. Buy a recent one. The market is changing fast.

11

HOW TO INVEST IN GOLD

a. WHY INVEST IN GOLD?

If you keep your money in the bank, you get interest on your savings. If you buy stocks, you may be paid dividends. If you invest in a business, you may get a share of profits. Gold, on the other hand, does not provide any return on a regular basis on your investment.

Why, then, are we talking about gold as an investment? Why should small investors even bother to consider gold as part of an investment program?

To understand the importance of gold as a form of investment, you need to understand the price history of gold:

Year	Average Price Per Ounce	% Increase
1968	$39	—
1973	$98	151%
1978	$193	395%
1982	$376	865%
1987	$447	1046%
1994	$381	877%

People buy gold for capital gains! They expect the gold price to move up with inflation.

You need more than $200 today to buy the same goods and services that could have been bought for less than $100 in 1977. One ounce of gold today will buy more goods and services than it probably did in 1977. In other words, when inflation hits, currencies are devalued, but gold increases in value. In recent years, the price of gold has increased at a much higher rate compared to the rate of inflation. Gold is considered to be the unofficial universal money. Since gold has an enormous potential to move ahead of inflation, any investment program should probably include gold.

One caution — gold has kept pace with inflation over a period of time, but don't forget that gold prices are volatile. This means the price of gold could go down in the short run and stay at that level for quite some time. A small investor must make sure not to invest any money in gold that might be needed in an emergency.

Until recently, an investor needed a substantial amount of money to invest in gold. However, currently there are opportunities for investors with just $100.

b. SOME COMMON WAYS TO PARTICIPATE IN THE GOLD MARKET

There are several ways in which an investor can participate in the gold market. Not all methods are suitable for the small investor. I will first discuss some of the common methods used, and then identify those that are suitable for the small investor.

There are basically six ways in which an investor can participate in the gold market. These are:

(a) Gold bullion (gold bars)

(b) Gold coins

(c) Gold certificates

(d) Gold stocks

(e) Gold options

(f) Gold futures

1. Gold bullion

Gold bullion is simply a gold bar. Gold bars are produced in a wide variety of sizes, ranging from five grams to 400 ounces. The gold prices quoted in the newspapers refer to the price per ounce for a standard 400-ounce gold bar. If you buy smaller bars, costs will be higher, since a bar charge is added to the standard price quoted. Bar charges can be in excess of 10% of the standard price.

2. Gold coins

There are two types of gold coins — bullion type and numismatic type.

Bullion coins are gold coins that have a value determined, to a large extent, by their gold content. These coins trade at a very small premium over their actual price in relation to their gold content. Here are some of the more popular bullion coins:

Country of Origin	Name of Coin	Gold Content
Canada	Maple Leaf	1 Ounce
United States	American Eagle	1 Ounce
United States	Double Eagle	1 Ounce
Australia	Golden Nugget Koala	1 Ounce
Austria	Corona	.96 Ounce
China	Panda	1 Ounce
France	Britannia Napoleon	1 Ounce
Mexico	Centenario	1.2056 Ounce
South Africa	Krugerrand	1 Ounce

Other bullion coins include the British sovereign (which has a higher premium), the Mexican 20, 10, 5 and 2 ½ peso coins, the Russian chevronetz and the South African ½, ¼, and ¹⁄₁₀ rand coins. Maple Leaf, Golden Nugget Koala, Britannia Napoleon, and American Eagle also have ½-, ¼-, and ¹⁄₁₀-ounce versions.

78

Numismatic gold coins are those minted at a certain point in time and are currently available in limited quantities. They sell at a premium that may be considerably higher compared to their gold content.

The price of these coins is determined by several factors. Some of the major factors are the following:

(a) Number of coins originally minted

(b) Number of coins still in circulation

(c) Age of the coin

(d) Condition of the coin

Coins minted in limited quantities with limited current circulation and older coins in better condition will, in general, have a greater value than coins minted in large quantities with a large number still in circulation, or more recently minted coins in poor condition.

While this may sound logical, it can be difficult to evaluate these factors. How do you know the number of coins currently in circulation? How is good condition defined? A simple blemish in a numismatic coin, which may not be apparent to the buyer, may lower the value of a numismatic coin considerably.

3. Gold certificates

Gold certificates are issued by some banks and dealers. When you buy gold certificates you are, in effect, buying gold bullion. The company that sells you these certificates stores the gold on your behalf. The bullion is registered in your name. The commission charges could be as low as $1/4$% or as high as 5%. In addition, the issuing company will charge you a modest storage fee. You can buy and sell gold this way without ever taking delivery. In many cases, you will avoid bar charges which you are expected to pay when you actually take delivery. You can also buy gold certificates through stock exchanges. For example, gold is traded on the Montreal Exchange like stocks and can be bought through your broker.

4. Gold stocks

Buying shares in gold mining companies is another way you can participate in the gold market. There are several South African and Canadian mining companies whose shares are commonly traded. Some investors prefer not to buy South African gold stocks because of the current political situation there. Some of the factors that affect the stock prices are the current price of gold, the cost of production per ounce, the life of the mine, and management competence.

5. Gold options

A gold option is a contract that gives you the right to buy (or sell) gold at a certain price before a certain date. You do not, however, have an obligation to buy or sell. For example, suppose the price of gold today is $400. You may buy an option contract that gives you the right to buy 100 ounces of gold within the next nine months (you can buy options with different lifespans) at, say, $425. This contract may cost you about $2,000 or a premium of about $20 per ounce. In the next nine months, if the price of gold rises much above $445 ($425 + $20 premium), your option will be worth a lot more than $2,000. For example, if gold moves up to $500, your option could be worth $7,500. You can realize the gain by selling the option back. The risk is that if the gold price remains below $545 for the next nine months, you will lose *all* your investment ($2,000).

6. Gold futures

A futures contract obligates you to buy (or sell) a certain amount of gold at some specific time in the future at a price specified now. You may, however, liquidate the contract before that date. Gold futures are usually for 100 troy ounces. You may buy a futures contract if you expect the price of gold to rise before a specified date.

The main attraction of gold futures is that you pay only about 10% to 20% of the total value when you buy the contract. The rest is due when you take delivery. This gives you high leverage if the market moves according to your predictions. Since you are obligated to buy (or sell) at a given price, you could end up losing a lot more than your original investment if the market moves against you.

c. HOW YOU CAN INVEST IN GOLD

Of the six basic ways of owning gold, two are completely unsuited for the small investor: gold futures and gold options. Both these methods can be very profitable. However, the small investor should avoid the temptation. When you buy options, you can lose all your investment capital; when you buy futures, you can lose all your investment capital plus a lot more. Since the small investor's priority is to preserve the capital, options and futures are unsuitable.

The following methods are better suited for the small investor.

1. Gold bullion for the small investor

Until recently, the smallest gold bullion bar that could be purchased was a one-ounce bar. Such bars carry a premium of 10%, in addition to an assaying fee. They are also difficult to trade.

Some brokerage houses in the United States offer accounts that work like mutual funds. For example, you may want to invest $100 in gold. Your investment is pooled with that of other investors. Gold bullion is bought in bulk each day. The commission can be about 6% (or less if you invest more). Such plans do not carry a storage fee, assaying fee, insurance fee, or sales tax. The gold is retained by the brokerage house and you can sell it whenever you want.

2. Gold coins for the small investor

As discussed earlier, there are two types of gold coins — bullion type and numismatic type. Bullion coins are traded solely for their gold content. Numismatic coins are traded not only for their gold content but also for qualities such as rarity, age, condition, appearance, etc. The premium on numismatic coins can far exceed their gold value. The value of numismatic coins may often be unrelated to their gold content. Therefore, numismatic gold coins cannot be truly considered as gold investments.

There are several bullion coins. The most popular of these are the South African Krugerrand, the Canadian Maple Leaf, the U.S. Eagle, and, to a lesser extent, the Chinese Panda and the Mexican Onza.

(a) The Krugerrand

The Krugerrand contains exactly one troy ounce of gold. It has a fineness of .9167 or 22 karats. It is widely traded and carries a premium of 2% to 6% over the gold price. Krugerrands are traded throughout the world. The Krugerrand is legal tender in South Africa.

Smaller investors may be interested to know that Krugerrands are also available in fractional units. You can buy ½ oz., ¼ oz., or ⅒ oz. Krugerrands. However, these fractional units carry a much higher premium, as shown here:

Unit	Typical Premium
1 oz. Krugerrand	4%
½ oz. Krugerrand	8%
¼ oz. Krugerrand	12%
⅒ oz. Krugerrand	18%

Thus, if gold is selling at $400, buying ten ⅒ oz. Krugerrand will cost you about $60 more than buying a 1 oz. Krugerrand. For this reason, you should not buy fractional units unless you cannot afford to buy the 1 oz. Krugerrand.

(b) The Maple Leaf

The Canadian Maple Leaf also contains exactly one troy ounce of gold. It has a fineness of .999 or 24 karats. Although a late-comer to the scene, it is now widely accepted around the world. It carries a premium similar to that of the Kruger-rand.

The 1 oz. Maple Leaf has a face value of $50 and is available in fractional units: ¼ oz. ($10 face value), and ¹⁄₁₀ oz. ($5 face value). The fractional units, as discussed before, carry a higher premium and hence are not recommended for the very small investor.

(c) The U.S. Eagle

The U.S. Eagle contains exactly one ounce of gold. It is very popular in the United States. The Eagle is available in smaller denominations as well: ½ oz., ¼ oz., and ¹⁄₁₀ oz. The premium is slightly higher compared to that of the Maple Leaf.

(d) The Mexican Onza

This coin is similar to those described above. It contains one troy ounce of gold. Although less widely traded, the Mexican Onza carries a premium similar to that of the Krugerrand or the Maple Leaf.

(e) The Austrian and the Hungarian Crown

The 100 crown (Corona) coins produced by Austria and Hungary are much more popular than their other gold coins. The 100 Corona contains .9802 ounces of fine gold, making it slightly less valuable as bullion than the Krugerrand or the Maple Leaf. Corona coins are not legal tender. They are copies of coins issued by the former Austro-Hungarian Empire. The Austrian and the Hungarian Coronas are usually considered to be the same coin, and trade at the same price. The dealer premium for these coins is relatively low.

(f) Austrian ducats

These coins contain less gold and claim a much smaller share of the market. The premium on these coins could be about 8% over their gold value.

(g) The Mexican peso

Of all gold coins issued by Mexico, the 50-peso coin is the most popular. It contains 1.2057 ounces of fine gold. It was originally issued in 1921 to commemorate Mexico's 100th anniversary and therefore is also called the Centenario. In South America, the Centenario is the most popular gold coin. The coin is also traded in North America and in Europe. All Centenarios are dated copies of the original issue.

The Mexican 20-peso, which contains .48 ounces of gold, is somewhat less popular.

(h) The British Sovereign

This coin contains .2354 ounces of fine gold. It has been minted continuously since 1817. These are semi-numismatic coins, especially those minted in earlier years. Some coins carry premiums of up to 50% over their gold bullion value. The British Sovereign bears the image of the reigning Queen or King on one side and a scene of St. George slaying the dragon on the other. It is also legal tender in Britain. The sovereign is popular with both investors and numismatists.

(i) U.S. $20 Gold Double Eagles

These coins were stuck between 1950 and 1933. Two types of Double Eagles are now in circulation — St. Gaudens and Liberty Head. These coins contain .97 troy ounces of gold and carry premiums up to 100%. These coins should be purchased in strictly uncirculated condition. However, even minted-state coins may bear "bag marks" (scratches) from being handled in bags.

3. Gold bullion accounts

A gold bullion account is exactly like a savings account, except that deposits are converted into ounces of gold at the time of deposit. The value of your "savings" is determined by the daily prices of gold. (Please note these savings do not pay any interest; your gain or loss is solely determined by the price of the gold on the day you decide to sell.)

4. Gold funds

Another way to participate in the gold market is to buy shares in gold mining companies. For a beginning investor, this has several disadvantages:

(a) Relatively high cost of quality mining stocks

(b) Commission for both buying and selling

(c) Possibility of a particular company being mismanaged

(d) Political climate affecting a particular company

A beginning investor needs an alternative that offers diversification, is cheaper, is safe, and carries no commissions. In fact, there is such an alternative. These are mutual funds that specialize in gold. These funds invest in gold (and other metals). Here are some such funds:

United States

- Benham Gold Equities Index
- Blanchard Precious Metals
- Bull & Bear Gold Investors Limited
- Fidelity Select American Gold / Precious Metals
- INVESCO Strategic Portfolio — Gold
- Lexington Goldfund
- Scudder Gold
- USAA Gold

- U.S. Gold Shares
- U.S. World Gold
- Vanguard Specialized Portfolio — Gold and Precious Metals

All the above are no-load funds.

Canada

In Canada, there are two no-load gold mutual funds:

Royal Trust Precious Metals
Royal Trust Investment Services Inc.
1st Floor, Mutual Funds
630 Rene Levesque Boulevard West
Montreal, Quebec
H3B 1S6
1-800-463-3863

(Minimum Investment: Initial: $500; Subsequent: $25)

Scotia Precious Metals Fund
c/o Scotia Investments
1 Richmond Street West
7th Floor
Toronto, Ontario
M5H 3W2
(416) 866-4574

(Minimum Investment: Initial $500; Subsequent: $50)

12

HOW TO INVEST IN SILVER

a. WHY INVEST IN SILVER?

There are several reasons why a beginning investor should consider silver.

(a) Silver is poor man's gold. In the spring of 1994, you could have bought 70 ounces of silver for the price of 1 ounce of gold.

(b) Silver often rises in price when gold goes up.

(c) Silver is an industrial metal. There is always a demand for silver.

(d) Unlike gold, silver is used in many industries. So the price of silver should rise in the long term.

b. SOME COMMON WAYS TO PARTICIPATE IN THE SILVER MARKET

As with gold, there are six basic ways to participate in the silver market. These are:

(a) Silver bullion

(b) Silver coins

(c) Silver certificates

(d) Silver stocks

(e) Silver options

(f) Silver futures

These ways of buying silver are exactly the same as their gold counterparts. For an explanation of the above methods, please refer to the chapter on gold.

c. HOW YOU CAN INVEST IN SILVER

Investing in silver is similar to investing in gold. Most dealers who deal in gold deal in silver.

1. Silver bullion

You can pay cash and accept delivery of silver bullion. Common sizes of silver bars are 10 (troy) ounces, 100 ounces, and 1,000 ounces. Since there are several charges when you take delivery, you may be better off leaving the silver you purchase with your dealer until you decide to sell. One large dealer of silver is:

Thomas Cooke Currency Services Inc.
630 Fifth Avenue
New York, NY 10111
(212) 757-6915

Thomas Cooke Group Canada Limited
10 King Street East
Toronto, Ontario
M5C 1C3
(416) 863-1611

2. Silver coins

Silver coins are perhaps the best starting point for small investors interested in precious metals. Until 1965, the United States produced silver coins in several denominations: dollars, half dollars, quarters, and dimes. Such coins are referred to as *junk silver* and are now bought and sold mainly for their silver content.

Junk silver can be bought as bags or as rolls. A bag contains silver coins whose face value is $1,000. The silver contents of pre-1965 coins is approximately 720 ounces per bag. Each bag will cost approximately 720 x the current silver price per ounce. The high price makes it difficult for small investors to invest in bags. Rolls are a lower cost alternative. Dimes come in rolls of 50, and quarters come in rolls of 40. The approximate cost is:

Dime rolls = 3.6 x the price per oz. of silver
Quarter rolls = 7.2 x the price per oz. of silver

There are also numismatic silver coins. For the beginning investor, however, junk silver still offers the best value. There are far too many silver coins from around the world that qualify for the title numismatic and are best left out of your portfolio until you become familiar with this market.

Junk silver can be bought from most of the coin dealers listed in the Resource Directory.

3. Silver bullion accounts

A silver bullion account works exactly like a gold bullion account (see chapter 11).

13

HOW TO INVEST IN REAL ESTATE

a. REAL ESTATE AND THE SMALL INVESTOR

You can make a fortune in real estate. But you need to be knowledgeable in buying a property and willing to spend the time to understand the market. I assume you do not want to spend a lot of time and that you do not want to get seriously involved in the real estate business. Even so, you can make money in a small way in real estate.

Get into real estate by all means, but only if you have some special knowledge. The reason for this is that real estate is highly leveraged. This means that you borrow a lot more than you currently have. If you buy a property for $100,000 and put down $10,000, you have borrowed $90,000. The only way you can make money is for the value of the property to go up. If it does not, you are paying interest on $90,000 year after year. This is not a position you want to be in if you are a small investor. So, I believe that small investors should not get into direct real estate investment unless they have some special knowledge in this area or know how to buy an undervalued property, add value to it by renovating, and then resell it. Since I don't expect most small investors to possess such special knowledge, I recommend you explore ways to profit from real estate.

If at all possible, you should own your own home. Owning your home commits you to paying the mortgage, but you save on rent. If the value of your house goes up, you can make a tidy profit. In Canada, you do not pay capital gains tax when you sell your home. This makes owning your home very attractive. It is an investment you can keep using for your benefit until there is profit to be made.

b. REAL ESTATE INVESTMENT TRUSTS (REITs)

REITs are companies that invest in apartment complexes, shopping malls, and other commercial and residential properties. When you buy shares (units) in these companies, you become a part-owner of this property.

Here are some REITs currently operating in Canada:

- RealFund

- Counsel

- CREIT

- Lantower

In the United States, there are two types of REITs: REITs that actually own properties and REITs that lend money to real estate developers. REITs that own properties (equity-type) have tax advantages and therefore should be preferred to the mortgage-type REITs. (In Canada there are hardly any REITs.)

Shares in REITs can generally be bought or sold like shares in any corporation. If you are interested in this form of investment, write to:

National Association of REITs
1129, 20th Street N.W.
Suite 305
Washington, DC 20036
(202) 785-8717

If you want to receive a list of REITs and would like to know more, request their REIT Fact Book and a current REIT list from the Association. (There may be a small charge for this.)

c. WHY INVEST IN REITs?

REITs normally aim to hold high quality real estate. REITs pass on all income (untaxed) to unit holders. While you need to pay tax on the income you receive, you may also be eligible for preferential tax treatment (such as capital cost allowance and interest deductions). REITs provide instant diversification and professional management.

d. WHAT ELSE SHOULD YOU KNOW?

You should remember that investing in REITs does not automatically mean that you will make money. Much depends on the experience of management and economic conditions when you invest. Another thing you should know is that not all REITs are equally liquid, especially if the properties held by an REIT are not of good value. So do your homework and find out what is in their portfolio before you invest. If you are not sure, don't invest. Look for other options.

e. HOW TO BUY AND SELL REIT UNITS

REIT units are like stocks. To buy them, you should go through your stockbroker.

f. REAL ESTATE MUTUAL FUNDS

There are also mutual funds that invest in real estate (mostly commercial). They work exactly the same way as many other mutual funds. There are some differences though:

- The value of a real estate mutual fund is decided by an evaluation of the properties owned by the mutual fund. Evaluations and what one actually would get for a property are often two different things.

- Many real estate mutual funds evaluate their net asset value only once in three months. This makes buying and selling less immediate.

- Real estate funds can impose a moratorium on redemptions if they feel redemptions will harm the fund even further when the market is down.

If you are still interested, here are some no-load real estate mutual funds:

United States

- Fidelity Real Estate Investment
- PRA Real Estate Securities
- US Real Estate (Load 0.1% redemption fee)

Canada

- MD Realty A
- MD Realty B
- Royal Lepage Commercial

14

EVEN MORE WAYS TO MAKE MONEY

So far, we have discussed different types of investments that are safe for a small investor. There are, however, several other forms of investments that are highly profitable. These investments share one or more of the following characteristics:

(a) You need a *larger amount of money* to participate.

(b) You need greater *knowledge or experience* to participate.

(c) There are several *pitfalls* for the unwary investor.

Some of these investments are presented here. Because these investments can be quite complex, please consult other sources before investing your money.

a. HOW TO MAKE MONEY IN OPTIONS

1. Call option

A *call option* is the right to buy 100 shares of a specified stock, at a specified price before a specified date. The stock specified is the *underlying stock*; the price at which you have a right to buy is the *strike price*; the particular date on which your right to buy expires is the *expiration date.*

For example, IBM shares traded at $57.50 on May 18. Suppose you expect the price to move up to at least $65 before July 22. Since it is too expensive to buy 100 shares of IBM ($57.50 x 100 = $5,750), you may buy a call option for about a $175 premium which gives you the right to buy 100 shares before July at $60 per share.

94

Since you have already paid a premium of $1.75 per share ($175 ÷ 100), IBM has to move up to at least $61.75 before July 22 for you to make a profit (strike price + premium: $60 + $1.75 = $61.75). Beyond this break-even point, every dollar move-up results in a profit of $100 to you. Thus, on the expiration day, if IBM sells at $65, your profit will be $600 on an investment of just $175. This is a profit of nearly 200% in just four months! You may sell your option at the current market price at any time you wish.

What happens if IBM trades at or below $61.75 on the expiration date? You simply lose all the money you paid for the option — $175 plus commission. You cannot, however, lose more than this amount.

2. Put option

You can also buy a *put* option. A put option gives you the right to sell 100 shares of a particular stock at a specified price before a specified date. In the above example, if you predicted that IBM would go down by July, you would buy a put option. You would make money if the stock went down below the strike price. Otherwise, you would lose the premium paid.

3. The advantages of options

Options are attractive for these reasons:

- You can participate in the growth of high price stocks with very little capital.

- Your maximum loss is pre-determined.

The main disadvantage of options is that if your prediction does not materialize before the expiration date, you stand to lose all your investment plus commission.

However, there are several ways in which an option can be used effectively. For example, suppose on May 14 you buy 100 shares of IBM which trade at $55. You can sell a call option which expires next July for, let's say, $275. This gives the buyer of the call option the right to buy from you 100 IBM shares at $55 before July 22. Between September and January, one of the following will happen.

(a) *IBM will go up steeply.* Should this happen, you will be asked to sell your shares at $55 per share. You get to keep $275 paid to you as a premium. Your profit for four months is equal to:

$$\frac{\text{Premium received}}{\text{Your investment during the period}} = \frac{275}{5,500} = 5\%$$

A return of 5% (or approximately 20% a year) is thus guaranteed.

(b) *IBM will neither move up or down.* If the price of IBM remains more or less the same, you will not be asked to sell your shares. You keep the $275 you received and, upon expiry of the option, you can sell another option on the same stock for a future date. You can repeat the process and get steady income periodically. In addition, any dividend you receive is also yours to keep.

(c) *IBM will go down steeply.* Should this happen, you will not be asked to deliver the shares. However, should you wish to sell the shares and cut your losses before the expiration date, it would be safer to repurchase the option you sold before selling your shares.

Thus, the above strategy assumes a pre-determined rate of return on your investment in a steady or a rising market and slightly lowers your losses in a declining market. (Please note that this strategy also limits your maximum profits in a sharply rising market.)

The strategy is both simple and conservative. There are several interesting ways to make money in options while at the same time limiting your risk. If this investment interests you, you should read at least one good book on the subject. You may want to start with a primer such as *Getting Started in Options* by Michael C. Thomsett (published by John Wiley Ltd., Second edition: 1993).

Options are traded like stocks. Your stockbroker will be able to buy and sell options for you according to your requirements.

b. HOW TO MAKE MONEY IN COMMODITIES

Commodity futures are simply a way of betting. Suppose in May of 1994, wheat is selling at $3 a bushel. You are convinced that by September, the price of wheat will be at least $3.50 a bushel. There is someone else in the marketplace who believes that the price will go down by September, probably to $2.50 a bushel. So you bet against each other — you agree to buy 5,000 bushels of wheat from the other person in September for $3; the other person agrees to sell it to you at that price.

You figure that if your prediction is correct, you stand to make a profit of 50¢ a bushel or $2,500 in all; the other person similarly figures that if the price goes down to $2.50, he will make a profit of 50¢ per bushel or $2,500 in all. If the price moves in either direction, one of you will gain and the other will lose a corresponding amount. In either case, the losing player just pays the winning player the difference, instead of actually buying or selling the wheat in question.

Although that is not the only use of commodity futures, most commodity futures are traded as described above. In actual practice, commodity trading has the following features:

- You do not directly bet with another player, you bet through a commodity broker. The broker, in turn, goes through a commodity exchange which is a central clearing house.

- Commodity trading is available only for certain grain, currencies, metals, food products, etc. When you bet (buy or sell a contract), you may do so only for a standard quantity (e.g., 5,000 bushels of wheat).

- When you bet, you have to put down a margin amount (a certain percentage of the total value of the contract). If the market moves against you, you may be asked to put down more money.

You may get out of the contract before the due date. Your profit or loss at this point will be determined by the market price of the contract.

You may, if you wish, take delivery of the commodity after the due date.

Obviously, just as you can buy a contract when you think the price will go up, you can also sell a contract. In this case, you agree to deliver the commodity (or pay the difference between the market price and the contract price) at a specified date. When you sell a contract, you assume that the price of the commodity will go down and you can profit by purchasing the contract at a lower price.

1. Disadvantages of commodity trading

Commodity trading requires considerable discipline. Many beginners lose all their capital during the first year of trading. At a minimum, you should —

(a) be able to control your greed when things go your way,

(b) be able to sleep soundly when you lose a few hundred dollars in a matter of hours, and

(c) resist over-trading.

2. Advantages of commodity trading

Because of the low margin requirement in commodity trading, it is possible to make large sums of money with a small amount of investment capital.

Commodities are a lot more volatile than other forms of investments. It is possible to make a quick fortune in commodities.

The rewards of commodity trading are high. While devastating losses are possible, for a disciplined trader it need be no more risky than trading in stocks and bonds. If you want to fully understand how this market works, Todd Lofton's *Getting Started in Futures* is a good book on the subject (published by John Wiley Ltd., Second edition: 1993).

There are several commodity exchanges. In most exchanges, the contract sizes are large. There are, however, two exchanges that sell smaller contracts:

The MidAmerica Commodity Exchange
141 West Jackson Boulevard
Chicago, IL 60604
(312) 341-3000

The Winnipeg Commodity Exchange
500 Commodity Exchange Tower
360 Main Street
Winnipeg, Manitoba
R3C 3Z4
(204) 949-0495

Just as you need a stockbroker to trade in stocks, you need a commodity broker to trade in commodities. Most large brokerage houses also deal in commodities. It is unwise to deal in commodities if you have less than $5,000 to $10,000 as risk capital. Many commodity brokerage firms will not even deal with small investors.

One final piece of advice: if you are a small investor, start with grain futures where the losses are smaller. Avoid trading in metals, currencies, etc., until you have a sufficiently large amount of capital.

c. HOW TO MAKE MONEY IN ART AND COLLECTIBLES

Works of art and collectibles are risky as investments. They may decline in value drastically, you may not find a ready market when you want to sell them, and, unless you are careful, you may end up paying inflated prices when you buy.

On the positive side, art and collectibles are pleasurable to own. They may appreciate in value more than any of your other investments, and, if you invest wisely, it is unlikely that you will incur any great loss over a long period of time.

1. What to do

If you are interested in investing in art and collectibles, you should follow these guidelines:

(a) *Specialize*: Collectibles include art, antiques, Chinese ceramics, diamonds, books, stamps, and a variety of other items. Choose an area you feel comfortable with and get to know as much as possible about the field.

(b) *Buy what you like to own*: Since most collectibles tend to be long-term investments, you may have to live with what you bought. You might as well buy something that gives you pleasure while you have it.

(c) *Avoid fads*: Fads, by definition, change. Do not rush to buy fad items. Fads change quickly and you may be stuck with something that is worthless from an investment point of view.

(d) *Buy quality*: Quality items keep their value while non-quality items are unpredictable. Concentrate on quality.

(e) *Buy collectibles that have large markets*: Some collectibles are highly specialized and only a handful of investors are interested. This type of investment is highly illiquid. Avoid such collectibles.

(f) *Get a certificate of authenticity*: When you buy a collectible, get a dealer's certificate of title, guarantee of authenticity, and registration.

(g) *Know the current market price before buying*: To avoid costly impulse purchases, you should investigate the current price range for the collectible you want to buy. You should also decide in advance the maximum price you are willing to pay.

(h) *Buy through reputable dealers*: Because fakes and worthless collectibles abound in the marketplace, try to buy only through reputable dealers.

2. How to get started

Sotheby's and Christie's are two of the most reputable auction houses for collectibles. Both of these firms publish catalogues through the year, giving detailed descriptions of the items that will be available at forthcoming auctions. These catalogues give the estimated prices of the items. You may send in your bid for any item you like. At the time of auction, the company will bid on your behalf so that, if you are successful, you will get the best possible price. You may wish to contact:

Sotheby's
1334 York Avenue
New York, NY 10021
(212) 606-7000

Sotheby's (Canada) Inc.
9 Hazelton Avenue
Toronto, Ontario
M5R 2E1
(416) 926-1774

Christie's Fine Art Auctioneers
170 Bloor Street West
Toronto, Ontario
M5S 1T9
(416) 960-2063

Christie's Fine Art Auctioneers
502 Park Avenue
New York, NY 10022

d. HOW TO MAKE MONEY IN TAX SHELTERS

We pay taxes on a graduated scale. As your income increases, you keep less and less of the additional money you earn. Although, overall, you may pay only 25% or 30% of your income as taxes, the marginal tax rate could be 40% or higher. This means that, at your level of income, you have to pay at least $40 in taxes for every extra $100 you earn.

For an investor this above fact is very important. Suppose you can save $3,000 a year. If you do not have to pay taxes on this, then you have $3,000 to invest. If you could get an 18% return on this amount, your savings would be worth more than $1 million in 25 years.

On the other hand, if you were to pay taxes at 40% on your savings of $3,000 a year, the total value of your investment at the end of 25 years would be $400,000 less. By planning your finances properly, you can reduce your tax bill, thus making more money available for your investments. Legal ways of avoiding taxes are usually referred to as tax shelters.

Tax shelters are usually of two types: *tax deferred* and *tax-free*. Tax deferred investments enable you to postpone the taxes to a future date, while tax-free investments enable you to avoid taxes completely. Both these types of investments should be considered seriously. If they apply to you, you should take advantage of them.

Several readers have written to me with their comments and suggestions since the first edition of this book. I have tried to respond to their suggestions in this edition. I have been unable to respond as fully as I would like to requests from readers for information on tax shelters. I am unable to include much information on taxes because tax rules can change very rapidly. What I write may become outdated by the time you read the book.

My general suggestion is to make use of tax shelters and retirement plans such as RRSP (Canada), IRA and Keogh (United States) whenever you can. My only caution is that *you should not invest in just anything because it is a tax shelter*. If it is not a sound investment, it is not a good buy just because it shelters your money from taxes.

Because taxes can affect the value of your investments, make sure you read some good books on the subject. Be sure that the books you read are not outdated. I urge you to find out as much as you can because this is a very important topic for small investors.

How do you compare tax-free investments with taxable investments? Let's say, for example, that a tax-free investment yields a 6% return and a taxable investment yields a 10% return. Which one should you choose? To compare the two, do the following calculation:

$$100 - \frac{\text{(Tax-Free Yield)}}{\text{(Taxable Yield)}} \times 100$$

In our example:

$$100 - \frac{6}{10} \times 100 = 40\%$$

This means your *marginal* tax (the tax you pay on the last dollar you earn) should be at least 40%, for it to be worthwhile.

e. HOW TO MAKE MONEY WITH SWISS BANK ACCOUNTS

A Swiss bank account is not just for the rich. It offers so many advantages that it is suitable even if you are a small investor. Let us consider some of the advantages.

1. Security

Swiss currency is one of the strongest in the world. In most countries the rate of inflation is so high it erodes the purchase power of the money you save. In Switzerland, on the other hand, the rate of inflation has been traditionally low.

2. Privacy

There are strict laws governing the secrecy of your account. In Switzerland, it is illegal for a bank to divulge information about your account to anyone, including the Swiss government. (This, however, may not protect a customer when he or she indulges in fraudulent activities).

3. Services

Swiss banks provide a wide variety of services to their customers. Unlike our banks in North America, Swiss banks can help you convert your currencies into Euro currency, buy stocks and bonds on your behalf, store gold and silver, and perform similar financial management services. The range of services offered by Swiss banks is indeed impressive.

4. Swiss bank account

Although many Swiss banks require a large minimum amount to open an account, some cater to small investors. To get started, write to the banks listed in the Resource Directory under Swiss Banks, and ask for an application to open a Swiss franc savings account. Once you open an account, you can mail checks drawn on a U.S. or Canadian bank. All correspondence can be conducted in English.

15

LOW-RISK STRATEGIES FOR HIGHER PROFITS

Most investors look for two things —

- safety of their capital, and
- increased return on their investments.

You can use specific strategies to get what you want. A strategy is a method that is well thought out in advance. You follow the strategy, even when things don't seem rosy. A strategy helps you avoid panic reactions when things don't go your way.

a. STRATEGY 1: DOLLAR COST AVERAGING

Let us suppose that —

(a) you want to invest a specific amount on a regular basis,

(b) you want to invest over a long period of time, and

(c) you are interested in high quality, dividend-paying stock.

There is no guarantee that the stocks will increase in value over any given period of time. For example, assume that in 1970 you bought $1,000 worth of stocks in each of the following ten prominent companies. Their worth on January 2, 1980, was:

Name of company	Stock value in 1970	Stock value in 1980
IBM	$1,000	$ 883
Sears	$1,000	$ 589
U.S. Steel	$1,000	$ 778
Westinghouse	$1,000	$ 692
General Motors	$1,000	$ 723
General Foods	$1,000	$ 809
Woolworth	$1,000	$ 665
Texaco	$1,000	$ 942
Eastman Kodak	$1,000	$ 584
Goodyear	$1,000	$ 419
	$10,000	$7,084

Ignoring the dividends for the time being, the investment is worth 30% *less* than it was ten years ago. (If you take inflation into account, the investments are worth less than 50% of the 1970 value).

During the 1987 stock market crash, the value of many stocks plummeted. Suppose you had bought blue chip stocks immediately after the crash. After three years (October, 1990) would your investment have appreciated sharply? The answer is no!

Thus, it is clear that even if you invest in blue chip companies, you need a good strategy to protect your investments.

Dollar cost averaging is one of the most widely known systems, and it achieves superior results under certain conditions. This system works best when you invest in high quality dividend-paying stocks on a regular basis.

Dollar cost averaging involves purchasing the same dollar amount of stock at regular intervals, regardless of the price of the stock at the time of each purchase. For example, you may decide to buy $1,000 worth of TD Bank shares each year. Suppose you had done this for ten years, e.g., 1971 to 1980.

AMOUNT INVESTED = $1,000 per year

Year	Share price	Shares bought	Total no. shares	Estimated dividends
1971	$12.31	81	81	$30.00
1972	$15.92	63	144	$63.00
1973	$19.38	56	200	$100.00
1974	$17.38	58	258	$158.00
1975	$19.75	51	309	$216.00
1976	$18.63	54	363	$258.00
1977	$16.80	60	423	$321.00
1978	$21.25	47	470	$400.00
1979	$21.63	36	506	$614.00
1980	$32.00	31	537	$755.00
	$1,95.05			$2,915.00

Average share price = $195.05 10 years = $19.50

Total dividend received = $2,915.00

By investing the same amount regularly, you were able to buy more shares when the prices were low. At the end of ten years, the average price paid per share was only $19.50 although the share price was $32 on October 31, 1980. In addition, you also received nearly 30% of your capital ($2,915) back in dividends.

As time goes by, the dividends also become very important. For example, by the end of the tenth year, the dividend received from TD Bank is equal to 75% ($755) of the annual investment! You can, of course, increase the profit by re-investing the dividends in addition to making your regular investment.

- Dollar cost averaging is a system suitable for regular investors over a long period of time. It works best with dividend-paying, high quality stocks.

- The system involves investing the same amount in the same stock periodically.

- In general, it may be said that dollar cost averaging is a simple system based on sound principles and is suitable for regular long-term investing.

When you invest the same amount in mutual funds at regular intervals, you are in fact using the dollar cost averaging method indirectly.

b. STRATEGY 2: THE RIGS STRATEGY

RIGS is simply an automatic way of investing according to a formula. RIGS is a conservative long-term strategy for investing. By using this strategy, you can expect to earn approximately 14% to 16% per year (on average) on your long-term investments. (This is based on past experience with the strategy; it is not a guarantee.)

RIGS stands for Recession, Inflation, Growth, and Safety (or Speculation). The basis of this strategy is the observation that economic conditions go in cycles and different investments do well under different economic conditions. During inflationary times, real estate, gold and other tangibles do well; during recessionary periods bonds, cash, and cash equivalents do well, and during growth periods, stocks and real estate do well. RIGS uses the following investments:

R-type investments

- Bonds
- Mortgage-backed securities
- Cash
- Cash equivalents

I-type investments

- Gold
- Real estate

108

- Other tangibles

G-type investments

- Common stocks
- Real estate

Some investors try to predict what is likely to happen in the future and invest accordingly. This can be risky when predictions go wrong. The RIGS strategy tries to avoid the risk by assuming that the future is not predictable, but even so money can be made. The strategy works as follows:

(a) Divide your money into three equal parts. (Example: You have $9,000 to invest. Divide it into three parts of $3,000 each).

(b) Invest one-third of your money in R-type investments.

(Example: Invest $3,000 in bonds or income mutual funds.)

(c) Invest one-third of your money in I-type investments.

(Example: Invest $3,000 in gold, silver, real estate or in mutual funds that invest in any of these investments).

(d) Invest one-third of your money in G-type investments. (Example: Invest $3,000 in stocks or equity mutual funds.)

(e) Whenever you have money to invest during the year, invest an equal amount in each type of investment (R,I, and G). If you save monthly, rotate your investment among the three types.

(f) At the end of the year, some of these investments would have gone up; some would have gone down. (Example: Let us assume that, by the year end, R-type investments are worth $3,600, I-type investments

$2,900, and G-type investments are worth $3,400, for a total of $9,900.)

(g) Rearrange your investments so that each type is worth the same dollar amount. (Example: Your investments are worth $9,900 by the year-end. You rearrange your investments so that each type — R, I, and G — has the same dollar value: $3,300. You do this by selling some of the R- and G-type investments and buying some I-type investments to bring every investment to the same dollar value.)

Once set up, this strategy needs very little attention. It works because it forces the investor to sell high and buy low every year. This strategy works well in the long term. It will not make money every single year, but when you take any five years (approximately one business cycle), the RIGS strategy has performed consistently well. By using this strategy, you can expect to make around 14% to 16% per year over a five-year period. This is not a guarantee, but a reasonable expectation based on past experience. You may occasionally find that all three investments have gone down. There is no need to panic. The investments will resume their growth soon enough.

The Investors Association of Canada has a special report called *RIGS: The Strategy for Investing*, which explains in simple terms what the strategy is, how it works, and how you can set up your own investment program. You can get a copy of this brief report from IAC for $12.95 plus $2 for postage. Write to:

Investors Association of Canada
26 Soho Street, Suite 380
Toronto, Ontario
M5T 1Z7

16

TWO HIGHER-RISK STRATEGIES FOR HIGHER PROFITS

The profitability of some of the investments already discussed can be further increased by using a variety of special techniques. Although these techniques have the potential to increase your profits quite considerably, they usually require a large capital outlay to begin with. Hence, these systems should be used only when you have sufficient capital. You should also keep in mind that these are long-term strategies.

The two strategies discussed in this chapter are based on switching between investments. They require some understanding of how financial markets work. You may find them useful halfway through your investment program. They are here only for your reference.

a. STRATEGY 1: STOCK MARKET — MONEY MARKET SWITCH

This strategy is based on the observation that whenever interest rates go down, the stock market goes up; conversely, whenever interest rates go up, the stock market goes down. While this relationship is not perfect, it is still strong enough for us to benefit by it.

There are several systems that take advantage of this relationship. One such system is described below:

(a) Calculate the 39-week moving average for a given stock market fund. (A 39-week moving average is simply the average price of the fund's share for the previous 39 weeks).

(b) If the current price of the fund is lower than the moving average, switch your money from the stock market fund to a money market fund.

(c) Continue plotting moving averages for the stock fund. When the current price of the stock fund goes above the moving average, switch all your investments back from the money market fund to the stock fund.

Following such a system increases the probability of being in the stock market when it is going up and being in the money market when the stock market is going down.

If you are interested in using such a system, but do not want to spend the time calculating moving averages, you may want to subscribe to one of the following newsletters which does the work for you and advises you when to switch. (Always call or write first and ask for a complimentary copy of the newsletter before subscribing.)

Fund Exchange
Paul A. Merriman and Associates
700-1200 Westlake Avenue North
Seattle, WA 98109-3530
(206) 285-8877

Telephone Switch Newsletter
P.O. Box 2538
Huntington Beach, CA 92647
(714) 536-2201

Switch Fund Timing
P.O. Box 25430
Rochester, NY 14625
(716) 385-3122

If you use this system, make sure that both your money market and stock market funds are run by the same group, that they are no-load funds, and that the funds offer telephone switching privileges.

b. STRATEGY 2: GOLD — SILVER SWITCH

The price of gold and silver usually goes up and down at the same time. Sometimes, however, the price of gold rises faster than silver; at other times, the price of silver rises faster than gold. The following table shows the price relationship between gold and silver over a four-year period.

	Gold price (per oz.)	Silver price (per oz.)	Number of oz. of silver per one oz. of gold
Year 1			
Quarter 1	$240	$ 8.66	28
Quarter 2	$281	$10.07	28
Quarter 3	$399	$20.61	19
Quarter 4	$524	$40.41	13
Year 2			
Quarter 1	$490	$14.50	34
Quarter 2	$662	$16.81	39
Quarter 3	$670	$20.70	32
Quarter 4	$589	$15.80	37
Year 3			
Quarter 1	$514	$11.95	43
Quarter 2	$421	$ 8.58	49
Quarter 3	$432	$ 9.04	48
Quarter 4	$400	$ 8.20	49
Year 4			
Quarter 1	$320	$ 7.07	45
Quarter 2	$314	$ 5.73	55
Quarter 3	$396	$ 8.20	48
Quarter 4	$442	$10.50	42

Thus, at the end of the first quarter of the first year, 28 ounces of silver bought one ounce of gold; at the end of the last quarter of the same year, as little as 13 ounces of silver bought one ounce of gold. Yet by the second quarter of the fourth year, one ounce of gold bought more than four times as much silver!

Because the silver-gold ratio has fluctuated historically, it is reasonable to expect that it will continue to do so in the future.

To capitalize on this fact, you can set up a simple strategy. Simply keep the dollar value of gold and silver equal. This is best explained by an example. In this example, an investor buys $10,000 worth of gold and $10,000 worth of silver. Every three months the investor calculates the current values of gold and silver and readjusts the dollar amounts such that 50% of the total amount is invested in gold and the remaining 50% in silver. This is how it works:

First Quarter

Price of gold — $500 an oz.

Price of silver — $20 an oz.

Invest $10,000 in gold (10,000 ÷ 500) = 20 oz. of gold.

Invest $10,000 in silver (10,000 ÷ 20) = 500 oz. in silver.

Second Quarter

Price of gold — $600 an oz.

Price of silver — $15 an oz.

Now the value of the holdings is:

Gold — 20 oz. x $600 = $12,000

Silver — 500 oz. x $15 = $7,500
                            $19,500

The investor wants to keep 50% ($19,500 ÷ 2 = $9,750) in silver and 50% in gold. Accordingly, $2,250 worth of gold

($12,000 - $9,750) is exchanged for $2,250 worth of silver. At this stage the investor has:

$9,750 ÷ $600 = 16.25 oz. of gold

$9,750 ÷ $15 = 650 oz. of silver

Third Quarter

Price of gold — $700

Price of silver — $20

Value of holdings:

Gold — $700 x 16.25 oz. = $11,375

Silver — $20 x 650 oz. = <u>$13,000</u>

Total: $24,375

Once again the investments are re-arranged so that 50% of the total amount is invested in silver and the other 50% in gold.

By now it should be obvious how the system works. Because gold went up in price during the second month and silver went down, silver was cheap in relation to gold. Consequently, gold was exchanged for silver. Subsequently, silver went back to its initial price while gold continued to climb. The total profit is now $4,375. An investor who did not follow this procedure would have made a profit of $4,000 (i.e., $700 x 20 oz. + $20 x 500 oz. = $24,000), which is about 2% less profit. Over a number of years, that 2% difference would be substantial in terms of dollar amount.

This is, of course, an artificial example. If you apply the principle to the actual data given earlier, it would look like the chart on the next page:

Date	Gold (oz.)	Silver (oz.)
Year 1		
Quarter 1	41.7	1,155
Quarter 2	41.71	155
Quarter 3	50.7	981
Quarter 4	63.2	819
Year 2		
Quarter 1	43.7	1,477
Quarter 2	40.6	1,599
Quarter 3	45.0	1,457
Quarter 4	42.0	1,567
Year 3		
Quarter 1	39.2	1,687
Quarter 2	36.8	1,818
Quarter 3	37.4	1,788
Quarter 4	37.0	1,806
Year 4		
Quarter 1	38.5	1,740
Quarter 2	35.1	1,924
Quarter 3	37.5	1,809
Quarter 4	40.2	1,694

That is, over a period of four years, 1.5 ounces of gold were parlayed into 539 ounces of silver without adding any more money!

17

HOW TO GET INFORMATION
AT LOW OR NO COST

Investment books can be expensive. But there are several sources of free information. As a small investor, you should make use of them whenever possible. But please remember, if you write for information from people who want to sell you something (such as stockbrokers and insurance companies), you are likely to get telephone calls from them. If you do not want to buy what they are trying to sell, be firm and say no. They can be very persuasive!

Many financial writers and consumer columnists often mention free booklets on investments. Such publications are often advertised. Some of these are published by industry associations to promote the industry, some by large companies for prestige and others by companies that hope you will do business with them. They can be very useful but not necessarily unbiased. Throughout this book, I have referred to several publications. In this chapter, I would like to give you the names of some useful publications that can be obtained free of charge.

Not all free publications are good, *but some of them are excellent*. In fact, some of the best information included in this book came to my attention through free publications. How do you tell a good publication from a bad one? It's not easy. All I can say is, do not get carried away by what you read. Do not feel that you will miss a golden opportunity unless you act as these publications tell you. *Opportunities will always be there for an intelligent investor.* As you gain experience, you will be able to discard bad advice.

In the meantime, use these publications to educate yourself at no cost. Exposure to different publications — even if some of them are bad — will make you a better investor.

a. U.S.-BASED MUTUAL FUNDS

You can get a number of free brochures on mutual funds from:

The Investment Company Institute
1401 H Street N.W.
Washington, DC 20005
(202) 326-5800

Here are some of the free brochures offered:

- *What is a Mutual Fund? 8 FUNDamentals*

- *Planning for College?* (12 pages)

- *A Close Look at Closed-End Mutual Funds* (12 pages)

- *Reading the Mutual Fund Prospectus* (28 pages)

- *A Translation: Turning Investment-ese into Investment Ease* (20 pages)

For $8.50, you can also get *Guide to Mutual Funds*, which contains fund names, addresses, telephone numbers (many toll-free), each fund's assets, initial and subsequent minimums, fees charged, where to buy, and other details. The introductory text serves as a short course in mutual fund investing.

The Mutual Fund Education Alliance (The Association of No-Load Funds) publishes *Investors Guide to Low-Cost Mutual Funds,* which costs $5. This directory includes 2,750 mutual funds listed by category and includes (for each fund) investment objectives, assets, minimum investment requirements, fees (if any), expense ratios and total return for one-, five-, and ten-year total returns. You may contact:

Mutual Fund Education Alliance
1900 Erie Street, Suite 120
Kansas City, MO 64116
(816) 471-1454

b. CANADIAN MUTUAL FUNDS

In Canada, The Investment Fund Institute of Canada has several brochures available to the investing public free of charge.

- *Answers to the 10 Most Asked Questions About Mutual Funds*
- *Capitalizing on Taxation*
- *Making Your RRSP Work Better For You*
- *Savings and Investments — There is a Difference*
- *Introducing Investment Funds*

In addition, you can also receive, on a quarterly basis, the performance of most Canadian mutual funds. These *Performance Tables* show one-, three-, five-, and ten-year performance figures for hundreds of Canadian mutual funds. Also free is the *Member Directory*, which is actually the names, addresses, and phone numbers of mutual fund companies that are members of the Investment Funds Institute of Canada. If you would like to receive an information package, please contact:

The Investment Funds Institute of Canada
151 Yonge Street, Suite 503
Toronto, Ontario
M5C 2W7
(416) 363-2158

c. OTHER PUBLICATIONS

The list given above is probably the most useful for the beginning investor. But a number of useful publications are available from other sources. A beginning investor should obtain these publications and become familiar with different aspects of investing.

Almost all stock exchanges have publications that are helpful to investors. The names and addresses of North American exchanges are given in the Resource Directory. You may want to write to them asking for any publication that will help the individual investor.

Many brokerage houses also publish information that is useful to individual investors. For example, Merrill Lynch in the United States has about 150 free brochures and booklets. The titles include:

- *The Catalogue of Investments*

- *How to Read a Financial Report*

- *You and Your Money*

- *The Bond Book*

You may want to contact:

Merrill Lynch Pierce Fenner & Smith, Inc.
Marketing Communications
800 Scudder's Mill Road
Plainsboro, NJ 08540-9019
1-800-637-7455
(212) 637-7455

Several industry associations also offer useful publications. For example the Certified General Accountants of Ontario offer free publications on taxation, executorship, and related topics. You may want to contact them for more information about the booklets that they make available to the general public:

CGA of Ontario
240 Eglinton Avenue East
Toronto, Ontario
M4P 1K8
(416) 322-6520

d. HOW TO GET EVEN MORE FREE PUBLICATIONS

The above list is by no means complete. There are literally hundreds of publications on investments available absolutely free. Not all of them are good. Some of them are very self-serving. A beginner may have difficulty distinguishing a good publication from a biased one. I would suggest that you get as many free publications as possible and go through them. But do not be in a hurry to act upon their suggestions. Gradually, you will be able to tell the facts from a mere sales pitch.

You can develop your own list of free publications through several sources:

(a) Regularly go through consumer columns in your daily newspaper; free publications are quite often mentioned in them.

(b) Go through the advertisements in the business section of your daily newspaper; free publications on investments are advertised in this section from time to time.

(c) Write to industry associations (e.g., No-load Mutual Funds Association, The Gold Institute, etc.), stock exchanges, etc. requesting information. You are likely to receive several useful publications.

PART IV
REALIZING YOUR DREAM:
FINANCIAL FREEDOM

18

FUNDAMENTALS OF FINANCIAL GROWTH

After reading this far, you might still be wondering how to achieve financial freedom on $5 a day. It is very well to list the available opportunities, but how exactly should a beginner go about devising a plan to achieve financial freedom? I will describe a typical plan to achieve financial freedom in the following chapter; but, before that, you need to understand some fundamentals of diversified long-term investments.

a. COMPOUND INTEREST

Even a modest amount, like $5 a day, when invested regularly over a long period of time, will gradually grow into a modest fortune. For example, $5 a day, invested at 15% return, will grow into $1 million in 35 years (see Chart #3).

Note how your savings grow slowly at the beginning and rapidly in later years. Time is an important element in making your money grow.

b. DIVERSIFIED INVESTMENTS

When your investments are diversified, the maximum you can lose on any one investment is 100%. The maximum gain, on the other hand is theoretically unlimited.

For example, if all you have is $10,000 in stocks, your stocks can go down in value and create losses for you. If, on the other hand, you have some stocks, some bonds, some gold, and some money market funds, it is very unlikely that all your investments will go down and stay down. As a matter of fact, when some types of investments are down, others tend to move up. For example, when interest rates go up, the price of bonds goes down, but you get to make more money in money market funds.

Another advantage of having diversified investments is that one of these investments may go up dramatically in the next ten to 15 years: for instance, gold quadrupled in value in the late seventies and early eighties; oil prices doubled during the Persian Gulf crisis in 1990. The stock market soared during the years 1982-87. The same holds true for the other investments that you build up. In a long-term diversified portfolio, the probability of growth is much greater than the probability of decline.

c. ECONOMIC CHANGES

Over a ten- to 15-year period, economic conditions change. Stock markets, gold, silver, foreign currencies, art, and collectibles go up and down. For example, during the 1984–85 year, bond prices went up by over 40%. By switching investments at appropriate times (see chapter 19), you can increase the return on investments appreciably.

d. CYCLES

The value of investments follows recurring patterns. At different points in time, different investments are favored by investors. These patterns are at times related to economic changes. While some people believe that such cycles can be predicted, long-term investors do not have to predict these. It is enough to know that cycles exist and to take advantage of the cycles when they occur.

e. FADS, PANICS, AND MASS HYSTERIA

From time to time, groups of people tend to act irrationally. Such irrationality and panic tend to dramatically increase the value of a specific investment to unreasonable levels for a

CHART #3
FUTURE VALUE — $150 SAVED MONTHLY
Interest compounded monthly

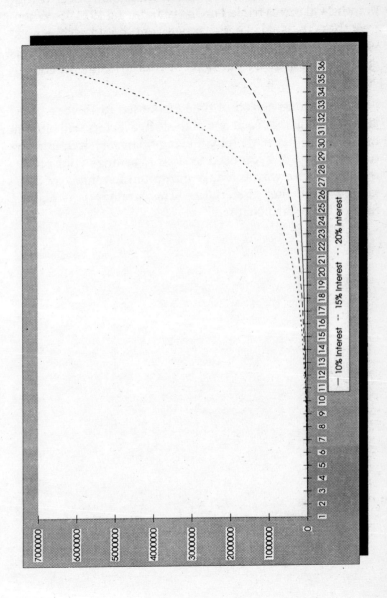

short period of time. If we just watch for these moments we can profit handsomely. For example, in 1979-1980, gold doubled in price in six weeks; silver tripled in price in four months! Oil prices tripled in one year during 1974-75. Whenever these unusual events happen, you should cash in most of your holdings and wait for prices to come down. This strategy will increase the value of your investments considerably.

Over a long period of time (about ten to 15 years), it is almost certain that each one of these five factors will operate in the marketplace, thereby making financial freedom a virtual certainty. All you need to do is to arrange your investments in such a way as to take maximum advantage of these factors when they materialize. This strategy is explained further in the next chapter.

19

A BLUEPRINT
FOR FINANCIAL FREEDOM

As mentioned earlier, even if you invest just $5 a day in the best possible way and do nothing else, you may be able to achieve financial freedom. But this will take a long time. If you wish to achieve financial freedom within a reasonable length of time (e.g., ten to 15 years), I suggest that you follow the example of Mr. Keen Investor given below.

Mr. Keen Investor has no savings but he is intelligent and keen. He is willing to put the principles explained in this book into practice. He is willing to increase his savings by 20% each year whenever he can. This is how he goes about doing it.

a.   PHASE 1: YEARS ONE TO THREE

Mr. Keen Investor is committed to saving $5 a day. In addition he is willing to add part of his annual salary increase, bonus, windfall money, unexpected savings, etc. He decides that every time his savings reach $100 he will invest it. This is what his calculations look like:

Year 1:	$5 a day to a total of $1,825 or approximately	18 x $100
Year 2:	$6 a day to a total of $2,190 or approximately	22 x $100
Year 3:	$7.20 a day to a total of $2,628 or approximately	26 x $100
		66 x $100

(Mr. Keen Investor figures that even if he can save only $5 a day during the second and third years, he can still add about 20% by other means.)

Mr. Keen Investor is conservative in his strategy and wants to diversify his investments without risking his capital. This is how he invests:

First	$100	Stock Funds	(SF)
Second	$100	Bond Funds	(BF)
Third	$100	Money Funds	(MF)
Fourth	$100	Foreign Funds	(FF)
Fifth	$100	Gold Funds	(GF)
Sixth	$100	Real Estate Funds	(RF)

After one year of saving $5 a day and investing it in the above program, his investments look like this:

SF	BF	MF	FF	GF	RF
$300	$300	$300	$300	$300	$300

This constitutes one block in Mr. Keen Investor's program. For the first three years, he decides to repeat investing in the same way. Thus, at the end of three years he expects his three blocks to look like the diagram below.

SF	BF	MF	FF	GF	RF
$300	$300	$300	$300	$300	$300
SF	BF	MF	FF	GF	RF
$360	$360	$360	$360	$360	$360
SF	BF	MF	FF	GF	RF
$440	$440	$440	$440	$440	$440

In other words, his investments are:

SF	BF	MF	FF	GF	RF
$1,100	$1,100	$1,100	$1,100	$1,100	$1,100

Although Mr. Keen Investor saved about $6,600 in the first three years, his investments have grown in value because of interest he has received from money market funds, dividends he has received from stock market and real estate funds, and a modest appreciation on his other investments, etc. He finds that some of these investments have appreciated modestly, some have depreciated modestly, some have appreciated considerably and so on. At the end of three years, his investments are worth $8,800.

b. PHASE 2: YEARS FOUR TO SIX

Mr. Keen Investor is now satisfied that he has a sound base from which to move to the second phase of the program. He decides to redistribute the $8,800 he has at this stage as follows:

Stock Funds	$2,000
Bond Funds	$2,000
Gold Funds	$1,000
Real Estate Funds	$1,000
Foreign Funds	$1,000
Money Funds	$1,000

He still has $800 left. He decides to invest this amount in more potentially rewarding (and risky) investments like art, collectibles, and call options.

In addition, Mr. Keen Investor continues his investment program by regularly investing an amount that is about 20% higher than the previous year. During the first three years, his block consisted of six units. From now on, Mr. Keen Investor decides to add one more unit to the block — risky investments (RI). His investment blocks for this phase look like this:

First	$100	Stock Funds (SF)
Second	$100	Bond Funds (BF)

Third	$100	Money Funds (MF)
Fourth	$100	Foreign Funds (FF)
Fifth	$100	Gold Funds (GF)
Sixth	$100	Real Estate Funds (RF)
Seventh	$100	Risky Investments (RI)

While continuing the basic program. Mr. Keen Investor decides that, by now, his investments are sufficiently diversified and he could increase his profits even more by using advanced techniques. The RIGS strategy (see chapter 15) especially appeals to him. He likes the fact that it is a safe and sensible strategy and very easy to use.

Regular savings, diversification, and the use of the RIGS technique help Mr. Keen Investor to achieve high returns on his investment. His total net worth at this point has increased to about $35,000. With this solid foundation, Mr. Keen Investor is ready to start the third phase of his investment program.

c. PHASE 3: YEARS SEVEN TO TEN

Mr. Keen Investor continues to save and invest regularly. He decides at this stage to continue to invest in high risk areas like commodity futures, art, collectibles, and options and sets aside $5,000 for this purpose.

He continues with the program and continues with the RIGS strategy. He speculates with some of his money, but has the bulk of his capital in solid investments. Mr. Keen Investor ignores day to day fluctuations in the value of his investments. He knows he is investing for the long haul and feels comfortable about his strategy.

As years go by, Mr. Keen Investor is very pleased with the results. Sometimes his investments are up, sometimes they are down. But there is no doubt that his plan has been working. His total average return on investment has exceeded 15% per year.

In addition, he has been able to take advantage of sudden price surges in gold, silver, etc. By the tenth year, his net worth has increased to more than $100,000.

He diligently continues investing while watching his systems make money for him. By the 15th year, Mr. Keen Investor has well over $300,000. "Well, I am financially independent now," he muses. "It is only a question of time — maybe five or six years — before I turn this into $1 million or more."

Not bad for someone who started with $5 a day 15 years earlier.

Now back to reality. The scenario described above has been constructed on the basis of historical rates of return on investments, taking into account the factors that affect investments over a ten- to 15-year period. You may, in the next 15 years, do much better or you may do somewhat worse, than he did. (It is unlikely that you will do much worse as long as you are a disciplined investor.)

In discussing Mr. Keen Investor, we have made some assumptions: he is able to increase his savings by 20% each year, he is aided at times by economic cycles, etc. Suppose you cannot increase your savings each year by 20%, or that you are hindered rather than helped by economic conditions? The answer simply is that these things do not matter in long-term disciplined investing. Economic conditions may delay the achievement of financial freedom by a few years, but they have no power to stop you from reaching your goal. (Please note that these comments do not apply to short-term investing).

Conversely, you may already have $7,000 or $8,000 to invest. In this case, you will be able to achieve your goal sooner.

Depending on your individual requirements, you may want to construct your investment blocks differently. No matter what you do, as long as you are disciplined, regular, and diversified in your investments, achieving financial freedom is a virtual certainty.

PART V
KEEPING TRACK OF YOUR PROGRESS

20

HOW TO START AND STAY ON COURSE

a. WATCHING YOUR PROGRESS

When you begin investing, your progress may not look very dramatic. For example, when you start investing $150 a month at 12%, at the end of the year you will have only about $100 more than you invested. If some investments go down temporarily, your return may look even worse. You may be tempted to give up your investment program. Don't. Remember this: Your investments always work slowly at the beginning. After a few years they gather momentum. It is important not to give up your program simply because it moves too slowly at the beginning.

As we saw earlier, money makes money and that money makes even more money. Suppose you stick with your investment program for a few years and accumulate $100,000. At this stage, the return on this amount would be $1,000 a month. But you cannot get there unless you are patient. If you follow the program outlined in this book, you will get there sooner or later.

There is another reason why your progress may seem slow. It is because you are too close to the action. It is like watching a child grow. If you attempt to watch a child grow everyday, it is difficult to know how fast that child is growing. The change is gradual and is not even noticeable on an everyday basis.

In any case, it is important to keep track of your progress. Keeping track forces you to make regular investments, and shows where your program's strengths and weaknesses are.

b. YOUR FINANCIAL FREEDOM WORKBOOK

You may want to consider the following format for creating your own "Financial Freedom Workbook":

(a) Buy a spiral notebook with ruled lines (8.5" x 11").

(b) On the first page, fill in the following information:

Your name: *Mr. Keen Investor*

Amount you can save
each day (or month):   *$150 per month*

Number of investments: *8*
                                        Stock Funds
                                        Bond Funds
                                        Money Funds
                                        Gold Funds
                                        Foreign Funds
                                        Real Estate Funds

(Please note that these are just examples. Feel free to create your own investment programs and rules. Whatever you do, you should feel comfortable about your plan. For example, if you don't want to buy gold bullion or put your money in a Swiss bank, don't. Instead buy something you are more comfortable with, such as stock market mutual funds. No matter what you decide, you should be determined to implement your plan.)

(c) Write down your investment plan.

Months	Amount	Investment
January/February	*$300*	*Stock Funds*
March/April	*$300*	*Bond Funds*
May/June	*$300*	*Money Market Funds*
July/August	*$300*	*Gold Mutual Funds*
September/October	*$300*	*Foreign Funds*
November/December	*$300*	*Real Estate Funds*

(d) Write down any ideas you have that will help you achieve financial freedom faster:

I will save at least 50% of all windfalls such as bonuses, tax refunds, pay increases etc.

If, in any given year, one of my investments rises in value by more than 30%, I'll sell about 20% and buy investments that have fallen in value.

(e) Use the Financial Freedom Worksheets (see Samples #1 and #2 on the following pages) as a model and create a worksheet for each of your investments. You should have one worksheet for each type of investment. For example, Mr. Keen Investor puts $150 in stock market funds twice a year. The "Total value" column of your worksheet shows you how your investment is performing month after month. Keeping such records serves two purposes: first, it shows how your investment has been doing, and second, it will come in handy during the tax season.

Over the years, you can create new worksheets to record your progress. This will be your "Financial Freedom Workbook."

In any case, you can start with the above and work through it for the first year. Then, you can modify the records to suit your purposes any way you like.

If you don't want to go to the trouble of creating your own record book, you can order your own "Financial Freedom Workbook" from the address below. This workbook comes with ready-to-use blank worksheets, as well as detailed instructions on how to record your program and a concise review of basic investment principles. Write to:

Standard Research Systems Inc.
380-26 Soho Street
Toronto, Ontario
M5T 1Z7

FINANCIAL FREEDOM WORKSHEET

MONTHLY WORKSHEET (USE A SEPARATE SHEET FOR EACH TYPE OF INVESTMENT)

YEAR 1993

INVESTMENT TYPE — STOCK MARKET FUND

	Previous Investments	January	February	March	April	May	June
Amount Invested	—	$150					
Market Value	—	$150	$180	$185	$195	$189	$185
Dividends	/						
Interest	/						
Total	—	$150	$180	$185	$195	$189	$185

	July	August	Sept.	October	Nov.	Dec.	Year End
Amount invested	$150						$300
Market Value	$335	$355	$385	$395	$375	$365	$365
Dividends							
Interest							
Total	$335	$355	$385	$395	$375	$365	$365
Notes on							

Transfer this to the Year-end Worksheet ←

SAMPLE #2
FINANCIAL FREEDOM YEAR-END WORKSHEET

YEAR-END WORKSHEET

YEAR 1993   Carried forward from last year   1

	PREVIOUS INVESTMENTS	Investment Type					
		STOCK MKT FUND	MONEY MKT. FUND	BOND FUND	FOREIGN FUND	REAL ESTATE FUND	GOLD FUND
Amount invested	1	$300	$300	$500	$300	$300	$300
Market Value	1	$365	$310	$340	$325	$250	$300
Dividends	1						
Interest	1						
Total	1	$365	$310	$340	$325	$250	$300

	Investment Type						
						Year end	
Amount invested						$1,800	
Market Value						$1,890	
Dividends							
Interest							
Total						$1,890	

← Transfer this to the 'previous investments' column for the next year.

Notes on Gain During the Year $1,890 - $1,800 = $90

Financial Freedom Workbook / Page

141

One workbook has enough space to record details of your investments for several years. During this time I hope you will achieve financial freedom — or at least be very close to it!

PART VI
RESOURCE DIRECTORY

HOW TO KEEP YOURSELF INFORMED

This book has most of the information you need to start investing. But, to be a successful investor, you should keep yourself informed at all times.

a. USEFUL PUBLICATIONS

1. Investors Association of Canada: *Money Digest*

If you are following the strategy outlined in this book, it is necessary for you to be an informed investor. Investors Association of Canada publishes a newsletter 12 times a year. *Money Digest* lists the best performing mutual funds, high-quality dividend-paying stocks, best GIC rates etc., along with informative articles written by experts. (You can get a free copy of *Money Digest* by completing and sending in the comment sheet at the end of the end of this book.) *Money Digest* is not available at newsstands and is distributed only to the members of Investors Association of Canada (IAC). I strongly recommend that you join the association. For more information write to:

Money Digest
Investors Association of Canada
380-26 Soho Street
Toronto, Ontario
M5T 1Z7

(a) Daily publications (for serious investors)

United States

- the *Wall Street Journal*
- the business section of any major daily newspaper such as the *New York Times*

145

Canada

- *Report on Business* (the *Globe and Mail*)
- *Financial Post*

(b) Weekly publications

United States

- *Barron's*

Canada

- *Financial Times*
- *Financial Post Weekly*

(c) Monthly publications

United States

- *Money*

Canada

- *MoneySaver* (11 times a year)

b. BOOKS

1. Investing in general

(a) For Canadian investors

- *Financial Pursuit* by Graydon Watters (published by FKI Financial Knowledge Inc., Toronto, revised 1994). An excellent book on financial planning.
- *How to Invest in Canadian Securities* (published by the Canadian Securities Institute, Toronto). A good introduction to investing in Canadian stock markets. Revised from time to time.

(b) For U.S. investors

- *Getting Started in Stocks* by Alvin D. Hall (published by John Wiley & Sons).

2. Mutual funds

(a) For Canadian investors

- *Understanding Mutual Funds* by Steven Kelman (published by Penguin Books, Toronto, 1993). A concise introduction to Canadian mutual funds. Revised from time to time.

- *The 1994 Buyer's Guide to Mutual Funds* by Gordon Pape (published by Prentice Hall, Toronto, 1993). A fund-by-fund listing of all mutual funds offered in Canada.

(b) For U.S. investors

- *Getting Started in Mutual Funds* by Alan Lavine (published by John Wiley & Sons, 1994).

- *Low-load Mutual Funds* (published annually by The Association of Individual Investors, Chicago).

3. Gold

- *The Gold Book* by Pierre Lassonde (published by Penguin Books, Toronto, 1993). Deals with all aspects of investing in gold. Also has a chapter on silver.

- *Investing in Gold* by Ned Goodman, Steven Kelman, and Johnathan Goodman (published by Key Porter Books, 1992).

4. Options

- *Option Strategies* by Courtney Smith (published by John Wiley, New York, 1987). One of the clearest introductions to various option strategies.

- *Getting Started with Options* by Michael C. Thomsett (published by John Wiley, 1993).

5. Real estate

- *Nothing Down for the '90s* by Robert G. Allen (published by Simon & Schuster, New York, 1990).

CANADIAN AND U.S. MUTUAL FUNDS

There are thousands of mutual funds in North America. Many hundreds of these are no-load funds (i.e., they charge no sales commission). *The funds listed here are no-load funds that require an initial minimum of no more than $500.* Once you become more familiar with mutual funds and increase your capital, you may want to explore other no-load funds that require a larger minimum. At that point, I suggest that you get information on other no-load funds by contacting other sources mentioned in this book.

In the following lists, "MIN" refers to the minimum investment required when you first join the fund; "SUB" refers to the minimum amount required if you subsequently want to add to your investment. All "1-800" numbers are toll-free.

a. CANADA-BASED FUNDS

1. Canadian equity funds (stock market funds)

- Associate Investors Limited
  Leon Frazer & Associates Ltd.
  8 King Street East, Suite 2001
  Toronto, Ontario
  M5C 1B6
  Phone: (416) 864-1120
  Fax: (416) 864-1491
  MIN: $100   SUB: None

- Batirente — Section Actions
  Batirente
  c/o St. Laurent Financial Corp.
  425, boul. de Maisonneuve Ouest
  Bureau 1740
  Montreal, Quebec
  H3A 3G5
  Phone: (514) 288-7545
  Fax: (514) 288-4280
  MIN: $500   SUB: $500

- CDA RSP Common Stock Fund
  Canadian Dental Association
  Retirement Savings Plan
  Canadian Dental Service Plans Inc.
  Suite 710 - 100 Consillium Place
  Scarborough, Ontario
  M1H 3G8
  Phone: (800) 561-9401
  Fax: (416) 296-8920
  MIN: $50   SUB: $25

- Camaf
  Canadian Anesthetists Mutual Fund Ltd.
  94 Cumberland Street, Suite 503
  Toronto, Ontario
  M5R 1A3
  Phone: (416) 925-7731
  Fax: (416) 920-7843
  MIN: $500   SUB: $10

- Canada Trust Investment Fund — Equity Part
  CT Mutual Fund Services Inc.
  Canada Trust Tower, BCE Place
  161 Bay Street, 3rd Floor
  Toronto, Ontario
  M5J 2T2
  Phone: (416) 361-8000
  Fax: (416) 361-5333
  MIN: None   SUB: None

- Cornerstone Canadian Growth Fund
  North American Trust Company
  Yonge Richmond Centre
  151 Yonge Street, 3rd Floor
  Toronto, Ontario
  M5C 2W7
  Phone: (416) 362-7211
  Fax: (416) 367-8483
  MIN: $500   SUB: $100

- Everest Special Equity Fund
  Everest Stock Fund
  CT Mutual Fund Services Inc.
  Canada Trust Tower, BCE Place
  161 Bay Street, 3rd Floor
  Toronto, Ontario
  M5J 2T2
  Phone: (416) 361-8000
  Fax: (416) 361-5333
  MIN: $500   SUB: NA

- First Canadian Equity Index Fund
  First Canadian Growth Fund
  First Canadian Special Growth Fund
  Bank of Montreal Investment Management Ltd.
  First Canadian Mutual Funds
  302 Bay Street, 8th Floor
  Toronto, Ontario
  M5X 1A1
  Phone: (416) 867-7670
  Fax: (416) 867-4728
  MIN: $500   SUB: $50

150

- Foresters Growth Fund — Equity
  Independent Order of Foresters
  789 Don Mills Road
  Don Mills, Ontario
  M3C 1T9
  Phone: (416) 429-3000
  Fax: (416) 429-6054
  MIN: $50   SUB: $50

- Great West Life Equity Index Inv. Fund
  Great West Life Equity Investment Fund
  Great-West Life Assurance Co.
  P.O. Box 6000
  Winnipeg, Manitoba
  R3C 3A5
  Phone: (204) 946-1190
  Fax: (204) 946-8622
  MIN: $100   SUB: $100

- Gyro Equity Fund
  Canadian Airline Pilots Association
  c/o Altamira Investment Services Inc.
  Suite 200 - 250 Bloor Street East
  Toronto, Ontario
  M4W 1E6
  Phone: (416) 925-1623
  Fax: (416) 925-5352
  MIN: $500   SUB: $100

- Hongkong Bank Equity Fund
  Hongkong Bank Securities Inc.
  #500-885 West Georgia Street
  Vancouver, B.C.
  V6C 3E9
  Phone: (604) 641-1999
  Fax: (604) 641-3044
  MIN: $500   SUB: $100

- InvesNat Equity Fund
  InvesNat Group of Funds
  c/o National Bank Securities Ltd.
  600 de la Gauchetiere Ouest
  Montreal, Quebec
  H3B 4L2
  Phone: (514) 394-8671
  Fax: (514) 394-8229
  MIN: $500   SUB: $50

- Montreal Trust Excelsior Funds: Equity Funds
  Montreal Trust Group
  Place Montreal Trust
  1800 McGill College Avenue, 12th Floor
  Montreal, Quebec
  H3A 3K9
  Phone: (514) 982-7000
  Fax: (514) 982-7069
  MIN: NA   SUB: NA

- Mutual Premier Blue Chip Fund
  Mutual Premier Growth Fund
  The Mutual Group
  c/o Mutual Diversico Ltd.
  227 King Street South
  Waterloo, Ontario
  N2J 4C5
  Phone: (519) 888-3863
  Fax: (519) 888-3646
  MIN: $500   SUB: $50

- National Trust Equity Fund
  National Trust
  1 Adelaide Street East, 7th Floor
  Toronto, Ontario
  M5C 2W8
  Phone: (416) 361-4541
  Fax: (416) 361-5563
  MIN: $500   SUB: $50

- O.I.Q. Ferique - Actions
  O.I.Q. Ferique
  c/o Ordre des Ingenieurs du Quebec
  2020 University, 18th Floor
  Montreal, Quebec
  H3A 2A5
  Phone: (514) 845-6141
  Fax: (514) 845-1833
  MIN: $500   SUB: $50

- OHA Canadian Equity Fund
  OHA Investment Management Ltd.
  150 Ferrand Drive
  Don Mills, Ontario
  M3C 1H6
  Phone: (416) 429-2661
  Fax: (416) 429-5945
  MIN: $500   SUB: $100

- OTG Investment Fund — Diversified Section
  OTG Investment Fund — Growth Section
  Ontario Teachers Group
  57 Mobile Drive
  Toronto, Ontario
  M4A 1H5
  Phone: (416) 752-9410
  Fax: (416) 752-6649
  MIN: $500   SUB: $50

- Royfund Canadian Growth Fund
  Royfund Equity Ltd.
  Royal Bank Management Inc.
  Royal Bank Plaza
  North Tower, 4th Floor, Box 70
  Toronto, Ontario
  M5J 2J2
  Phone: (416) 974-0616
  Fax: (416) 974-4076
  MIN: $100   SUB: $25

- Royal Trust Canadian Special Growth Fund
  Royal Trust Canadian Stock Fund
  Royal Trust Investment Services Inc.
  630 Rene Levesque Boulevard West
  1st Floor, Mutual Funds
  Montreal, Quebec
  H3B 1S6
  Phone: (800) 463-3863
  Fax: (514) 876-2762
  MIN: $500   SUB: $25

- Scotia Canadian Equity Growth Fund
  Scotia Mutual Funds
  c/o Scotia Securities Inc.
  1 Richmond Street West, 7th Floor
  Toronto, Ontario
  M5H 3W4
  Phone: (416) 866-4754
  Fax: (416) 866-2018
  MIN: $500   SUB: $50

- Strata Canadian Fund
  Strata Mutual Funds
  101 Frederick Street, 5th Floor
  P.O. Box 9032
  Kitchener, Ontario
  N2G 4R8
  Phone: (519) 888-5021
  Fax: (519) 888-5925
  MIN: $500   SUB: $50

- Tradex Equity Fund Limited
  Tradex Management Inc.
  Suite 504, 124 O'Connor Street
  Ottawa, Ontario
  K1P 5M9
  Phone: (613) 233-3394
  Fax: (613) 233-8191
  MIN: $500   SUB: $100

- Trust Pret & Revenu — Fonds Canadien
  Trust Pret et Revenu du Canada
  850 Place d'Youville
  Quebec City, Quebec
  G1R 3P6
  Phone: (418) 692-1221
  Fax: (418) 692-1675

2. U.S. Equity funds

- Cornerstone U.S. Fund
  See address and phone number under
  Canadian equity funds section
  MIN: $500   SUB: $100

- Everest AmeriGrowth Fund
  Everest U.S. Equity Fund
  See address and phone number under
  Canadian equity funds section
  MIN: $500   SUB: NA

- First Canadian U.S. Growth Fund
  See address and phone number under
  Canadian equity funds section
  MIN: $500   SUB: $50

- InvesNat American Equity Fund
  See address and phone number under
  Canadian equity funds section
  MIN: $500   SUB: $50

- Mutual Premier American Fund
  See address and phone number under
  Canadian equity funds section
  MIN: $500   SUB: $50

- National Trust American Equity Fund
  See address and phone number under
  Canadian equity funds section
  MIN: $500   SUB: $100

- Royal Trust American Stock Fund
  Royal Trust Zweig Strategic Growth Fund
  See address and phone number under
  Canadian equity funds section
  MIN: $500   SUB: $25

- Scotia American Equity Growth Fund
  Scotia CanAm Growth Fund
  See address and phone number under
  Canadian equity funds section
  MIN: $500   SUB: $50

- Trust Prêt et Revenu — Fonds Americain
  See address and phone number under
  Canadian equity funds section
  MIN: $500   SUB: $100

3. International equity funds

- Capstone International Investment Fund
  See address and phone number under
  Canadian equity funds section
  MIN: $500   SUB: $50

- Cornerstone Global Fund
  See address and phone number under
  Canadian equity funds section
  MIN: $500   SUB: $100

- Everest AsiaGrowth Fund
  Everest EuroGrowth Fund
  Everest International Fund
  Everest North American Fund
  See address and phone number under
  Canadian equity funds section
  MIN: $500   SUB: NA

- First Canadian International Growth Fund
  See address and phone number under
  Canadian equity funds section
  MIN: $500   SUB: $50

- Hongkong Bank Asian Growth Fund
  See address and phone number under
  Canadian equity funds section
  MIN: $500   SUB: $100

- InvesNat European Equity Fund
  See address and phone number under
  Canadian equity funds section
  MIN: $500   SUB: $50

- Montreal Trust Excelsior Funds: International
  See address and phone number under
  Canadian equity funds section
  MIN: NA   SUB: NA

- Mutual Premier International Fund
  See address and phone number under
  Canadian equity funds section
  MIN: $500　　SUB: $50

- OHA Foreign Equity Fund
  See address and phone number under
  Canadian equity funds section
  MIN: $500　　SUB: $100

- Royal Trust Asian Growth Fund
  Royal Trust European Growth Fund
  Royal Trust Japanese Stock Fund
  See address and phone number under
  Canadian equity funds section
  MIN: $500　　SUB: $25

- Scotia Global Growth Fund
  See address and phone number under
  Canadian equity funds section
  MIN: $500　　SUB: $50

4.　Specialty equity funds

- First Canadian Resource Fund
  See address and phone number under
  Canadian equity funds section
  MIN: $500　　SUB: $50

- National Trust Special Equity Fund
  See address and phone number under
  Canadian equity funds section
  MIN: $500　　SUB: $50

- Royal Trust Energy Fund
  Royal Trust Precious Metals Fund
  See address and phone number under
  Canadian equity funds section
  MIN: $500　　SUB: $25

158

- Scotia Precious Metals Fund
  See address and phone number under
  Canadian equity funds section
  MIN: $500   SUB: $25

5. **Balanced funds**

- Barreau du Quebec Fonds Placement - Equilibree
  Barreau du Quebec
  c/o Trust La Laurentienne
  425, boul de Maisonneuve Ouest
  Montreal, Quebec
  H3A 3G5
  Phone: (514) 284-7000
  Fax: (514) 284-7586
  MIN: None   SUB: None

- Batirente — Section Diversifiee?
  See address and phone number under
  Canadian equity funds section
  MIN: $500   SUB: $500

- CDA RSP Balanced Fund
  See address and phone number under
  Canadian equity funds section
  MIN: $50   SUB: $25

- Capstone Investment Trust
  See address and phone number under
  Canadian equity funds section
  MIN: $500   SUB: $50

- Cornerstone Balanced Fund
  See address and phone number under
  Canadian equity funds section
  MIN: $500   SUB: $100

- Everest Balanced Fund
  See address and phone number under
  Canadian equity funds section
  MIN: $500   SUB: NA

- F.M.O.Q. Fonds de Placement
  F.M.O.Q. Omnibus Balanced
  Fed. des Medecins Omnipracticiens du Quebec
  1440, rue Ste-Catherine Ouest, Suite 1100
  Montreal, Quebec
  H3G 1R8
  Phone: (514) 878-1911
  Fax: (514) 878-4455
  MIN: $500   SUB: $100

- First Canadian Asset Allocation Fund
  See address and phone number under
  Canadian equity funds section
  MIN: $500   SUB: $50

- Great-West Life Diversified RS Inv. Fund
  Great-West Life Equity/Bond Inv. Fund
  See address and phone number under

- Canadian equity funds section
  MIN: $100   SUB: $100

- Hongkong Bank Balanced Fund
  See address and phone number under
  Canadian equity funds section
  MIN: $500   SUB: $100

- InvesNat Retirement Balanced Fund
  See address and phone number under
  Canadian equity funds section
  MIN: $500   SUB: $50

- Montreal Trust Excelsior Funds: Balanced Fund
  Montreal Trust Excelsior Funds: Total Return Fund
  See address and phone number under
  Canadian equity funds section
  MIN: NA   SUB: NA

- National Trust Balanced Fund
  See address and phone number under
  Canadian equity funds section
  MIN: $500   SUB: $100

- O.I.Q. Ferique - Equilibre
  See address and phone number under
  Canadian equity funds section
  MIN: $500   SUB: $50

- OHA Balanced Fund
  See address and phone number under
  Canadian equity funds section
  MIN: $500   SUB: $100

- OTG Investment Fund
  See address and phone number under
  Canadian equity funds section
  MIN: $500   SUB: $50

- Royfund Balanced Fund
  See address and phone number under
  Canadian equity funds section
  MIN: $100   SUB: $25

- Royal Trust Advantage Balanced Fund
  Royal Trust Advantage Growth Fund
  See address and phone number under
  Canadian equity funds section
  MIN: $500   SUB: $25

- Scotia Stock & Bond Fund
  See address and phone number under
  Canadian equity funds section
  MIN: $500   SUB: $50

- Strata Tactical Fund
  See address and phone number under
  Canadian equity funds section
  MIN: $500   SUB: $50

- Trust Prêt et Revenu — Fonds de Retraite
  See address and phone number under
  Canadian equity funds section
  MIN: $500   SUB: $100

6. Preferred dividend funds

- Montreal Trust Excelsior Funds: Dividend Funds
  See address and phone number under
  Canadian equity funds section
  MIN: NA   SUB: NA

- National Trust Dividend Fund
  See address and phone number under
  Canadian equity funds section
  MIN: $500   SUB: $50

- Royfund Dividend Fund
  See address and phone number under
  Canadian equity funds section
  MIN: $100   SUB: $25

- Royal Trust Growth and Income Fund
  See address and phone number under
  Canadian equity funds section
  MIN: $500   SUB: $25

7. Mortgage funds

- CIBC Mortgage Investment Fund
  CIBC Securities Inc.
  P.O. Box 51
  Commerce Court Postal Station
  Toronto, Ontario
  M5L 1A2
  Phone: (416) 980-3863
  Fax: (416) 351-4438
  MIN: $500   SUB: $100

- Everest Mortgage Fund
  See address and phone number under
  Canadian equity funds section
  MIN: None   SUB: None

- First Canadian Mortgage Fund
  See address and phone number under
  Canadian equity funds section
  MIN: $500   SUB: $50

- Great-West Life Mortgage Investment Fund
  See address and phone number under
  Canadian equity funds section
  MIN: $100   SUB: $100

- InvesNat Mortgage Fund
  See address and phone number under
  Canadian equity funds section
  MIN: $500   SUB: $50

- Montreal Trust Excelsior Funds: Mortgage Fund
  See address and phone number under
  Canadian equity funds section
  MIN: NA   SUB: NA

- Mutual Premier Mortgage Fund
  See address and phone number under
  Canadian equity funds section
  MIN: $500   SUB: $50

- OTG Investment Fund - Mortgage Income Fund
  See address and phone number under
  Canadian equity funds section
  MIN: $500   SUB: $50

- Royfund Mortgage Fund
  See address and phone number under
  Canadian equity funds section
  MIN: $100   SUB: $25

- Royal Trust Mortgage Fund
  See address and phone number under
  Canadian equity funds section
  MIN: $500   SUB: $25

- Scotia Mortgage Fund
  See address and phone number under
  Canadian equity funds section
  MIN: $500   SUB: $50

- Trust Pret & Revenu - Fonds "H"
  See address and phone number under
  Canadian equity funds section
  MIN: $500   SUB: $100

8. Bond/mortgage funds

- CDA RSP Bond & Mortgage Funds
  See address and phone number under
  Canadian equity funds section
  MIN: $50   SUB: $25

- National Trust Mortgage Fund
  See address and phone number under
  Canadian equity funds section
  MIN: $500   SUB: $50

- Scotia Income Fund
  See address and phone number under
  Canadian equity funds section
  MIN: $500   SUB: $50

b. U.S.-BASED FUNDS

1. Aggressive growth funds

- Berger One Hundred
  P.O. Box 5005
  Denver, CO 80217
  Phone: 1-800-333-1001, (303) 329-0200
  MIN: $250   SUB: $50

- MIM Stock Appreciation
  4500 Rickside Road, Suite 440
  Cleveland, OH 44131
  Phone: 1-800-233-1240, (216) 642-3000
  MIN: $250   SUB: $50

- Prudent Speculator
  P.O. Box 75231
  Los Angeles, CA 90075
  Phone: 1-800-444-4778, (213) 778-7732

- Twentieth Century Gifttrust
  Twentieth Century Growth
  Twentieth Century Ultra
  Twentieth Century Vista
  4500 Main Street
  P.O. Box 419200
  Kansas City, MO 64141
  Phone: 1-800-345-2021, (816) 531-5575
  MIN: None   SUB: $25

2. **Growth funds**

- AARP Capital Growth
  P.O. Box 2540
  Boston, MA 02208
  Phone: 1-800-253-2277,(617) 439-4640
  MIN: $500   SUB: None

- American Pension Investors — Growth
  P.O. Box 2529
  2303 Yorktown Avenue
  Lynchburg, VA 24501
  Phone: 1-800-544-6060, (804) 846-1361
  MIN: $500   SUB: $100

- Armstrong Associates
  750 North St. Paul
  Lock Box 13, Suite 300
  Dallas, TX 75201
  Phone: (214) 720-9101
  MIN: $250   SUB: None

- Beacon Hill Mutual
  75 Federal Street
  Boston, MA 02110
  Phone: (617) 482-0795
  MIN: None   SUB: None

- Century Shares Trust
  One Liberty Square
  Boston, MA 02109
  Phone: 1-800-321-1928, (617) 482-3060
  MIN: $500   SUB: $25

- Fidelity Retirement Growth
  82 Devonshire Street
  Boston, MA 02109
  Phone: 1-800-544-8888, (801) 534-1910
  MIN: $500   SUB: $250

- GE U.S. Equity
  3003 Summer Street
  Stamford, CT 06905
  Phone: 1-800-242-0134
  MIN: $500   SUB: $100

- MIM Stock Growth
  See address and phone number under aggressive
  growth funds section
  MIN: $250   SUB: $50

- MSB Fund
  330 Madison Avenue
  New York, NY 10017
  Phone: (212) 551-1920
  MIN: $50   SUB: $25

- National Industries
  5990 Greenwood Plaza Boulevard
  Englewood, CO 80111
  Phone: (303) 220-8500
  MIN: $250   SUB: $25

- Nicholas
  700 N. Water Street, #1010
  Milwaukee, WI 53202
  Phone: 1-800-227-5987, (414) 272-6133
  MIN: $500   SUB: $100

- Rainbow
  255 Park Avenue, Suite 209
  New York, NY 10169
  Phone: (212) 983-2980
  MIN: $300   SUB: $50

- Schroder US Equity
  787 Seventh Avenue
  New York, NY 10019
  Phone: 1-800-344-8332, (212) 841-3841
  MIN: $500   SUB: $100

- Sentry
  1800 N. Point Drive.
  Stevens Point, WI 54481
  Phone: 1-800-533-7827, (715) 346-7048
  MIN: $200   SUB: $50

- Twentieth Century Heritage
  Twentieth Century Select
  See address and phone number under aggressive
  growth funds section
  MIN: None   SUB: $25

- Volumetric
  87 Violet Drive
  Pearl River, NY   10965
  Phone: 1-800-541-3863, (914) 623-7637
  MIN: $500   SUB: $200

3. Growth and income funds

- AARP Growth & Income
  See address and phone number under growth
  funds section
  MIN: $500   SUB: None

- Amana Income
  1300 N. State Street
  Bellingham, WA 98225
  Phone: 1-800-728-8762
  MIN: $100   SUB: $25

- Babson Growth
  Three Crown Center
  2440 Pershing Road, #G-15
  Kansas City, MO 64108
  Phone: 1-800-422-2766, (816) 471-5200
  MIN: $500   SUB: $50

- Berger One Hundred & One
  See address and phone number under aggressive
  growth funds section
  MIN: $250   SUB: $50

- Charter Capital Blue Chip Growth
  4920 West Vilet Street
  Milwaukee, WI 53208
  Phone: (414) 257-1842
  MIN: $50   SUB: $50

- MIM Stock Income
  See address and phone number under aggressive
  growth funds section
  MIN: $250   SUB: $50

- Salomon Brothers Investors
  7 World Trade Centre, 38th Floor
  New York, NY 10048
  Phone: 1-800-725-6666, (212) 783-1301
  MIN: $500   SUB: $50

4. **Balanced funds**

- Evergreen Foundation
  2500 Westchester Avenue
  Purchase, NY 10577
  Phone: 1-800-235-0064, (914) 694-2020
  MIN: $500   SUB: None

- Lepercq-Istel
  1675 Broadway, 16th Floor
  New York, NY 10019
  Phone: 1-800-338-1579, (212) 698-0749
  MIN: $500   SUB: 1 share

- MIM Bond Income
  See address and phone number under aggressive
  growth funds section
  MIN: $250   SUB: $50

- PAX World
  224 State Street
  Portsmouth, NH 03801
  Phone: 1-800-767-1729, (603) 431-8022

- Strong Investment
  Strong Total Return
  P.O. Box 2936
  Milwaukee, WI 53201
  Phone: 1-800-368-1030, (414) 359-1400
  MIN: $250   SUB: $50

- Twentieth Century Balanced
  See address and phone number under aggressive
  growth funds section
  MIN: None   SUB: $25

- Vanguard Star
  Vanguard Financial Center
  P.O. Box 2600
  Valley Forge, PA 19482
  Phone: 1-800-662-7447, (215) 648-6000
  MIN: $500   SUB: $100

5. **International stock funds**

- Twentieth Century International Equity
  See address and phone number under aggressive
  growth funds section
  MIN: None   SUB: $25

c. **BOND FUNDS (CANADIAN)**

- Barreau du Quebec Fonds Placement - Obligations
  See address and phone number under balanced
  funds section
  MIN: None   SUB: None

- Batirente - Section Obligations
  See address and phone number under
  Canadian equity funds section
  MIN: $500   SUB: $500

- Canada Trust Investment Fund - Income Part
  See address and phone number under
  Canadian equity funds section
  MIN: NA   SUB: NA

- Cornerstone Bond Fund
  See address and phone number under
  Canadian equity funds section
  MIN: $500   SUB: $100

- Everest Bond Fund
  See address and phone number under

- First Canadian Bond Fund
  First Canadian International Bond Fund
  See address and phone number under
  Canadian equity funds section
  MIN: $500   SUB: $50

- Great-West Life Bond Investment Fund
  See address and phone number under
  Canadian equity funds section
  MIN: $100   SUB: $100

- Gyro Bond Fund
  See address and phone number under
  Canadian equity funds section
  MIN: $500   SUB: NA

- InvesNat Short-Term Government Bond Fund
  See address and phone number under
  Canadian equity funds section
  MIN: $500   SUB: $50

- Montreal Trust Excelsior Funds: Income Fund
  See address and phone number under
  Canadian equity funds section
  MIN: NA   SUB: NA

- Mutual Premier Bond Fund
  See address and phone number under
  Canadian equity funds section
  MIN: $500   SUB: $50

- National Trust Income Fund
  See address and phone number under
  Canadian equity funds section
  MIN: $500   SUB: $50

- O.I.Q. Ferique - Obligations
  See address and phone number under
  Canadian equity funds section
  MIN: $500   SUB: $50

- OHA Bond Fund
  See address and phone number under
  Canadian equity funds section
  MIN: $500   SUB: $100

- Royfund Bond Fund
  Royfund International Income Fund
  See address and phone number under
  Canadian equity funds section
  MIN: $100   SUB: $25

- Royal Trust Bond Fund
  Royal Trust International Bond Fund
  See address and phone number under
  Canadian equity funds section
  MIN: $500   SUB: $25

- Scotia CanAm Income Fund
  Scotia Defensive Income Fund
  See address and phone number under
  Canadian equity funds section
  MIN: $500   SUB: $50

- Strata Government Bond Fund
  See address and phone number under
  Canadian equity funds section
  MIN: $500   SUB: $50

- Tradex Bond Fund
  See address and phone number under
  Canadian equity funds section
  MIN: $500   SUB: $100

- Trust Prêt et Revenu — Fonds d'Obligations
  See address and phone number under
  Canadian equity funds section
  MIN: $500   SUB: $100

d. BOND FUNDS (U.S.)

1. Corporate bond funds

- Nicholas Income
  See address and phone number under growth
  funds section
  MIN: $500   SUB: $100

2. Government bond funds

- Alliance Bond-U.S. Gov't "C"
  P.O. Box 1520
  Secaucus, NJ 07096
  Phone: 1-800-221-5672
  MIN: $250   SUB: $50

- Twentieth Century U.S. Gov'ts
  See address and phone number under aggressive
  growth funds section
  MIN: None   SUB: $25

3. Mortgage backed bond funds

- **AARP GNMA & U.S. Treasury**
  See address and phone number under growth
  funds section
  MIN: $500   SUB: $0

- **Alliance Mortgage Strategy "C"**
  See address and phone number under government
  bond funds section
  MIN: $250   SUB: $50

4. General bond funds

- **AARP High Quality Bond**
  See address and phone number under growth
  funds section
  MIN: $500   SUB: $50

- **Babson Bond Trust-Port L**
  See address and phone number under growth and
  income funds
  MIN: $500   SUB: $50

- **Pacifica Asset Preservation**
  237 Park Avenue, Suite 910
  New York, NY 10017
  Phone: 1-800-662-8417, (212) 808-3937
  MIN: $500   SUB: $50

- **Twentieth Century Long-Term Bond**
  See address and phone number under aggressive
  growth funds section
  MIN: None   SUB: $25

5. Tax-exempt bond funds

- **AARP Insured Tax Free General Bond**
  See address and phone number under growth
  funds section
  MIN: $500   SUB: $0

- Alliance Municipal Income — CA "C"
  Alliance Municipal Income — National "C"
  See address and phone number under government
  bond funds section
  MIN: $250   SUB: $50

- Dupree KY Tax-Free Income
  Dupree KY Tax-Free Short to Medium
  P.O. Box 1149
  Lexington, KY 40589
  Phone: 1-800-866-0614, (606) 254-7741
  MIN: $100   SUB: $100

- Pacifica Short Term CA Tax-Free
  See address and phone number under general
  bond fund section
  MIN: $500   SUB: $50

e. MONEY MARKET FUNDS (CANADIAN)

- Batirente — Section Marche Monetaire
  See address and phone number under
  Canadian equity funds section
  MIN: $500   SUB: $500

- CDA RSP Money Market Fund
  See address and phone number under
  Canadian equity funds section
  MIN: $50   SUB: $25

- Capstone Cash Management Fund
  See address and phone number under
  Canadian equity funds section
  MIN: $500   SUB: $50

- Colonia Money Market Fund
  Colonial Life Insurance Company
  2 St. Clair Avenue East
  Toronto, Ontario
  M4T 2V6
  Phone: (416) 960-3601
  Fax: (416) 323-0934
  MIN: $500   SUB: $50

- F.M.O.Q. Marche Monetaire
  See address and phone number under
  Canadian equity funds section
  MIN: $500   SUB: $100

- First Canadian Money Market Fund
  First Canadian T-Bill Fund
  See address and phone number under
  Canadian equity funds section
  MIN: $500   SUB: $50

- Great-West Life Money Market Inv. Fund
  See address and phone number under
  Canadian equity funds section
  MIN: $100   SUB: $100

- Montreal Trust Excelsior Funds: Money Market
  Fund
  See address and phone number under
  Canadian equity funds section
  MIN: NA   SUB: NA

- Mutual Money Market Fund
  See address and phone number under
  Canadian equity funds section
  MIN: $500   SUB: $50

- National Trust Money Market Fund
  See address and phone number under
  Canadian equity funds section
  MIN: $500   SUB: $100

- O.I.Q. Ferique — Marche Monetaire
  See address and phone number under
  Canadian equity funds section
  MIN: $500   SUB: $50

- OHA Short-Term Fund
  See address and phone number under
  Canadian equity funds section
  MIN: $500   SUB: $100

- OTG Investment Fund — Fixed Value Section
  See address and phone number under
  Canadian equity funds section
  MIN: $500   SUB: $50

- Prudential Money Market Fund
  Prudential Fund Management Canada Limited
  200 Consillium Place, 6th Floor
  Scarborough, Ontario
  M1H 3E6
  Phone: (416) 296-0777
  Fax: (416) 296-3186
  MIN: $300   SUB: $100

- Pursuit Money Market Fund
  Pursuit Financial Management Corp.
  1200 Sheppard Avenue East, Suite 402
  Willowdale, Ontario
  M2K 2S5
  Phone: (416) 502-9393
  Fax: (416) 502-9394
  MIN: $500   SUB: $50

- Royal Trust $U.S. Money Market Fund
  Royal Trust Canadian T-Bill Money Market Fund
  See address and phone number under
  Canadian equity funds section
  MIN: $500   SUB: $25

- Spectrum Savings Fund
  Spectrum Bullock Financial Services
  Suite 200 - 55 University Avenue
  Toronto, Ontario
  M5J 2H7
  Phone: (416) 360-2200
  Fax: (416) 360-2180
  MIN: $500   SUB: $25

- Strata Money Market Fund
  See address and phone number under
  Canadian equity funds section
  MIN: $500   SUB: $50

f. MONEY MARKET FUNDS (U.S.)

- Cigna Money Market Fund Inc.
  CIGNA
  1350 Main Street
  Springfield, MA 01103
  Phone: 1-800-562-4462, (413) 781-7776
  MIN: $500   SUB: $50

- Country Capital Money Market Fund
  Country Capital
  1701 Towanda Avenue
  Bloomington, IL 61701
  Phone: (309) 557-2444
  MIN: $100   SUB: $50

- Franklin Tax-Exempt Money Market Fund
  Franklin Federal Money Fund
  Franklin Group of Funds
  777 Mariners Island Boulevard
  San Mateo, CA 94404
  Phone: 1-800-632-2180, (415) 570-3000
  MIN: $500   SUB: $25

- Mariner Cash Management Fund
  Mariner Government Fund
  Mariner
  9003 Greenstree Commons, Suite 1
  Marlton, NJ 08053
  Phone: 1-800-632-2536, (609) 695-9300
  MIN: $100   SUB: $10

- MIMLIC Money Market Fund
  MIMLIC
  400 North Robert Street
  St. Paul, MN 55101-2098
  Phone: 1-800-443-3677, (612) 223-4252
  MIN: $250   SUB: $25

- Mutual of Omaha Cash Reserve Fund
  Mutual of Omaha
  10235 Regency Circle
  Omaha, NE 68114
  Phone: 1-800-228-9596, (402) 397-8555
  MIN: None   SUB: None

- Phoenix Money Market Series
  Phoenix
  101 Munson Street
  Greenfield, MA 01301
  Phone: 1-800-243-1574, (413) 774-3151
  MIN: $25   SUB: $25

- Rodney Square: Money Market Portfolio
  U.S. Government Portfolio
  Rodney Square
  Rodney Square North
  Willmington, DE 19890
  Phone: 1-800-225-5084, (302) 651-1923
  MIN: None   SUB: None

- Sigma U.S. Government Fund
  Sigma Money Market Fund
  Sigma
  3801 Kennett Park, Suite C-200
  Wilmington, DE 19087
  Phone: 1-800-441-9490, (302) 652-3091
  AND
  100 Oliver Street
  Boston, MA 02110
  Phone: 1-800-441-9490, (617) 268-7575
  MIN: $500   SUB: $100

- Transamerica Cash Reserve
  Transamerica
  P.O. Box 2598
  Los Angeles, CA 90051-1598
  Phone: (213) 741-7702
  MIN: $500   SUB: $100

g. DISCOUNT BROKERS

The following is a list of discount stockbrokers in Canada and
the United States.

1. Canada

- Toronto Dominion Greenline
  Geenline Investor Services Inc.
  P.O. Box #1, TD Centre
  Toronto, Ontario
  M5K 1A2
  (416) 982-7981, (416) 944-5467

Regional offices:

Ontario: 1-800-268-8209

Quebec: 1-800-363-1171

Atlantic: 1-800-565-0769

Manitoba: 1-800-665-8705

180

Saskatchewan: 1-800-667-6856

Alberta: 1-800-472-9717

Saskatoon: (306) 975-7398

Edmonton: (403) 448-8088

British Columbia: 1-800-663-0480

Windsor: 1-800-265-0846, (519) 252-7703

Local offices:

- 1791 Barrington Street, Suite 510
  P.O. Box 634
  Halifax, Nova Scotia
  B3J 2T3
  Phone: (902) 423-1171

- 2001 University, 19th Floor
  Montreal, Quebec
  H3A 2A6
  Phone: (514) 289-8439

- Royal Trust Tower
  77 King Street West, 16th Floor
  Toronto, Ontario
  M5K 1A2
  Phone: (416) 982-7686

- 100 King Street West, Suite 310
  Hamilton, Ontario
  L8P 1A2
  Phone: (905) 521-1073, 1-800-263-8560

- Talbot Centre, 11th Floor
  148 Fulerton Street
  London, Ontario
  N6A 5P3
  Phone: 1-800-265-4447, (519) 679-6440

- Minto Place Building
  427 Laurier Avenue
  P.O. Box 56088
  Ottawa, Ontario
  K1R 7Z1
  Phone: 1-800-267-8884, (613) 783-6322

- Suite 1617, 201 Portage Avenue
  Box 7700
  Winnipeg, Manitoba
  R3C 3E7
  Phone: (204) 988-2641

- 1874 Scarth Street, Suite 1280
  Regina, Saskatchewan
  S4P 4B3
  Phone: (306) 525-3370

- Home Oil Tower, T.D. Square
  #1100, 324 8th Avenue S.W.
  Calgary, Alberta
  T2P 2Z2
  Phone: (403) 292-2870

- Pacific Centre
  590 Howe Street
  Box 10261
  Vancouver, B.C.
  V7Y 1E8
  Phone: (604) 654-3783

- Bank of Montreal
  Investor Services
  302 Bay Street, 6th Floor
  M5A 1A1
  (416) 867-4000

- Scotia Discount Brokerage
  1 Richmond Street West
  Toronto, Ontario
  M5H 3W4
  Phone: (416) 866-2006

- Desjardins Securities
  2020 Université, 9th Floor
  Montreal, Quebec
  H3A 2A5
  Phone: 1-800-268-8471

2. **United States**

- Bidwell
  209 S.W. Oak Street
  Portland, OR 97204
  Phone: 1-800-872-0711, (503) 790-9000

- Muriel Siebert and Co.
  885 3rd Avenue, Suite 1720
  New York, NY 10022
  Phone: 1-800-547-6337, (212) 644-2400

- Burke Christensen & Lewis
  303 West Madison Street
  Chicago, IL 60606
  Phone: 1-800-621-0392, (312) 225-8283

- York Securities
  160 Broadway, East Bldg., 7th Floor
  New York, NY 10038
  Phone: (312) 349-9700

- Fidelity Brokerage Services Inc.
  82 Devonshire Street
  Boston, MA 02109
  Phone: 1-800-225-1799, (617) 570-7000

- Fleet Brokerage
  2 North Riverside Plaza, Suite 1717
  Chicago, IL 60606
  Phone: (312) 930-5879

- Pacific Brokerage Services
  5757 Wiltshire Boulevard, Suite 3
  Beverly Hills, CA 90036
  Phone: 1-800-421-8395, (213) 939-1100

- Quick & Reilly, Inc.
  26 Broadway, Lobby
  New York, NY 10004
  Phone: 1-800-221-5220, (212) 747-5000

- Charles Schwab and Co.
  101 Montgomery Street
  San Fransisco, CA 94104
  Phone: 1-800-472-4922, (415) 398-1000

h. NORTH AMERICAN STOCK EXCHANGES

The following is a list of North American stock and commodity exchanges.

1. Canada

- Alberta Stock Exchange
  300-5th Avenue S.W., 21st Floor
  Calgary, Alberta
  T2P 3C4
  Phone: (403) 974-7400

- Montreal Exchange
  800 Square Victoria, Box 61
  Montreal, Quebec
  H4Z 1A9
  Phone: (514) 871-2424

- Toronto Futures Exchange
  Toronto Stock Exchange
  The Exchange Tower
  2 First Canadian Place
  Toronto, Ontario
  M5X 1J2
  Phone: (416) 947-4700, (416) 947-4487

- Vancouver Stock Exchange
  Stock Exchange Tower
  P.O. Box 10333, 609 Granville Street
  Vancouver, B.C.
  V7Y 1H1
  Phone: (604) 689-3334

- Winnipeg Commodity Exchange
  500 Commodity Exchange Tower
  360 Main Street
  Winnipeg, Manitoba
  R3C 3Z4
  Phone: (204) 949-0495

- Winnipeg Stock Exchange
  1 Lombard Place, 29th Floor
  Winnipeg, Manitoba
  R3B 0Y2
  Phone: (204) 942-89431

2. **United States**

- American Stock Exchange (AMEX)
  86 Trinity Place
  New York, NY 10006
  Phone: 1-800-THE-AMEX, (212) 306-1000

- Boston Stock Exchange (BSE)
  One Boston Place
  Boston, MA 02108
  Phone: (617) 723-9500

185

- Chicago Board of Trade (CBOT)
  141 West Jackson Boulevard
  Chicago, IL 60605
  Phone: (312) 435-3500

- Chicago Board Options Exchange (CBOE)
  400 South LaSalle Street
  Chicago, IL 60605
  Phone: (312) 786-5600

- Chicago Mercantile Exchange (CME)
  30 South Wacker Drive
  Chicago, IL 60606
  Phone: (312) 930-1000

- Chicago Rice & Cotton Exchange
  141 West Jackson Street
  Chicago, IL 60604
  Phone: (312) 341-3078

- Chicago Stock Exchange
  440 South Lasalle
  Chicago, IL 60605
  Phone: (312) 663-2222

- Cincinnati Stock Exchange (CSE)
  36 East 4th, Suite 906
  Cincinnati, OH 45202
  Phone: (513) 621-1410

- Coffee, Sugar & Cocoa Exchange (CSCE)
  4 World Trade Center
  New York, NY 10048
  Phone: (212) 938-2900

- Commodity Exchange Inc. (COMEX)
  4 World Trade Center
  New York, NY 10048
  Phone: (212) 938-2900

- Kansas Board of Trade (KCBT)
  4800 Main Street, Suite 303
  Kansas City, MO 64112
  Phone: (816) 753-7500

- MidAmerica Commodity Exchange (MIDAM)
  141 West Jackson Boulevard
  Chicago, IL 60604
  Phone: (312) 341-3000, (312) 341-3078

- Minneapolis Grain Exchange (MGE)
  400 South Fourth Street
  130 Grain Ex. Building
  Minneapolis, MN 55415
  Phone: (612) 338-6212

- New York Cotton Exchange (NYCE)
  Phone: (212) 938-2650, (212) 938-2652
  New York Futures Exchange (NYFE)
  Phone: (212) 938-4940

- New York Mercantile Exchange (NYMEX)
  Phone: (212) 938-2222
  4 World Trade Center
  New York, NY 10048
  Phone: (212) 938-2222

- New York Stock Exchange (NYSE)
  11 Wall Street
  New York, NY 10005
  Phone: (212) 656-3000

- Pacific Stock Exchange (PSE)
  301 Pine Street
  San Fransisco, CA 94104
  Phone: (415) 393-4000

- Philadelphia Stock Exchange (PHLS)
  Philadelphia Board of Trade (PBOT)
  1900 Market Street
  Philadelphia, PA 19103
  Phone: (215) 496-5000, (215) 496-5165

i. SWISS BANKS

The following is a list of Swiss banks. Please note that many of these banks need a large minimum. If you are curious, you may want to write to some of these banks and request more information.

- Credit Suisse
  Paradeplatz 8
  P.O. Box 590
  8070 Zurich
  Switzerland
  Phone: 01-215-1111

- Foreign Commerce Bank
  Bellariastrasse 82
  8038 Zurich
  Switzerland
  Phone: 01-482-6688
  Mailing Address:
  P.O. Box 5022
  8022 Zurich

- Ueberseebank AG
  Limmatquai 2
  8024 Zurich
  Switzerland

- Bank Leu AG
  Badenerstrasse 244
  CH-8004 Zurich
  Switzerland

PRACTICAL TIME MANAGEMENT

How to get more things done in less time

by Bradley C. McRae

$7.95

Here is sound advice for anyone who needs to develop practical time management skills. It is designed to help any busy person, from any walk of life, use his or her time more effectively. Not only does it explain how to easily get more things done, it shows you how your self-esteem will improve in doing so. More important, emphasis is placed on maintenance so that you remain in control. Whether you want to find extra time to spend with your family or read the latest bestseller, this book will give you the guidance you need — without taking up a lot of your time!

Some of the skills you will learn are:

- Learning to monitor where your time goes
- Setting realistic and attainable goals
- Overcoming inertia
- Rewarding yourself
- Planning time with others
- Managing leisure time
- Finding time for physical fitness
- Planning time for hobbies and vacations
- Maintaining the new you

ORDER FORM

All prices are subject to change without notice. Books are available in book, department, and stationery stores. If you cannot buy the book through a store, please use this order form. (Please print.)

Name_____

Address_____

_____

Charge to: ❑Visa   ❑ MasterCard

Account Number_____

Validation Date _____

Expiry Date_____

Signature_____

❑Check here for a free catalogue.

IN CANADA
Please send your order to the nearest location:

Self-Counsel Press
1481 Charlotte Road
North Vancouver, B.C.   **OR**   4 Bram Court
V7J 1H1   Brampton, Ontario
                                                         L6W 3R6

IN THE U.S.A.
Please send your order to:

Self-Counsel Press Inc.
1704 N. State Street
Bellingham, WA 98225

YES, please send me:

_____copies of **Practical Time Management**, $7.95

Please add $3.00 for postage & handling.
Canadian residents, please add 7% GST to your order.
WA residents, please add 7.8% sales tax.

Visit our Internet Web site at *http://www.swifty.com/scp*